True Happiness

By Steve Preston

1st Edition

Table of Contents

Contents

Introduction

Are you happy? Has anyone ever told you they were they were filled with happiness so strong they could almost not believe it? This book will help you understand how, when, and what that could mean. It will provide you with insights concerning one of life's mysteries that you deserve to experience.

What is happiness?

Let me tell you right now happiness has nothing to do with health, money, coordination, looks, friends, success, love affairs, big muscles, or triumph. True happiness is not immediate nor is it always accomplished without some horrible times. To find out about this happiness thing, we will need to understand a number of things including Anthropic Science, life's dimensional qualities, what death is, how we can modify reality, why we live, what time is, Quantum Superposition, Relativity, discussions about the power of "positive thinking", the idea behind "Think and Grow Rich", vibrational matter and chakra, Self-Actualization and how to move mountains with faith the size of a grain of mustard-seed. I know it sounds complicated, but it is well worth it. This is not a religion book, but there will have to be some characteristics addressed from Biblical teaching along with the teachings of Abraham Maslow, Sigmund Freud, Albert Einstein, Milo Wolff, John Keely, John Hutchison, Napoleon Hill, Norman Vincent Peale, Lao Tzu, and many others. We will find life is different than you once believed and happiness can be more intense than you can imagine. Before we get into the meat of this, let me start off with a very strange verse in the Bible which we can call the "Lose to Gain" verse.

Lose to Gain

You are reading in the Bible and you come to a strange verse. After reading it a few times, it still sounds strange.

Matthew 16:24-17- For <u>whoever wants to save their life will lose it</u>, <u>but whoever loses their life for me will find it</u>. <u>What good will it be for someone to gain the whole world, yet forfeit their soul?</u>--- Or what can anyone give in exchange for their soul? -- "Truly I tell you, some who are standing here <u>will not taste death</u> before they see the Son of Man coming in his kingdom."-- After six days Jesus -- led them up a high mountain by themselves. There he was transfigured -- Just then there appeared before them <u>Moses and Elijah</u>, talking with Jesus.

This is the craziest thing someone could say. Saving your life by losing your life sounds bonkers. You read on and BAM! There it is again.

Mark 8:31-9:6- For <u>whoever wants to save his life will lose it</u>, but whoever loses his life for me and for the gospel will save it. <u>What good is it for a man to gain the whole world, yet forfeit his soul?</u> -- "I tell you the truth,

8

some who are standing here will not taste death before they see the kingdom of God come with power." After six days Jesus -- led them up a high mountain, where they were all alone. There he was transfigured --And there appeared before them Elijah and Moses, who were talking with Jesus.

Wait just a minute, once was silly; twice is absurd. Still further and the same thing is written again.

Luke 9:23-33-For whoever wants to save their life will lose it, but whoever loses their life for me will save it. What good is it for someone to gain the whole world, and yet forfeit their very self? --- "Truly I tell you, some who are standing here will not taste death before they see the kingdom of God." About eight days after Jesus -- took Peter, John and James -- and went up onto a mountain to pray. As he was praying, the appearance of his face changed, and his clothes became as bright as a flash of lightning. Two men, Moses and Elijah, appeared in glorious splendor, talking with Jesus. They spoke about his departure, which he was about to bring to fulfillment at Jerusalem.

Man oh man; if someone wanted to drive it into our head, repeating it over and over is making my head hurt! All 4 portions of all three verses say the same things.

1. To "truly live, you must separate yourself from this world or die to this world.
2. Gaining ANYTHING in this world is complete rubbish during life and especially after you die.
3. Some of the Disciples would see Jesus coming back to control the Earth while they were alive.

9

[This hasn't happened yet so we may think the people are getting really old.]

4. Elijah's and Moses' souls were still around and became "clothed" in flesh.

It doesn't seem to stop. Here is another.

Romans 8:13 *For if you live according to the flesh, you will die; but if by the Spirit you put to death the misdeeds of the body, you will live.*

Why should we die to live and what does this to do with happiness? Just to make you mad, I'm not telling you exactly what these verses mean concerning happiness more than what I stated above right now because <u>you have to understand who and what you are first</u> so you will have a guide to what makes you TRULY happy. For that let's look at something called Life Resonance.

Life Resonance

The next thing I want to put out there is something many of you have witnessed. When people are in a crowd, they start acting like the others in the crowd good or bad. Normal Vincent Peale described the effect as *"the power of positive thinking"*. The same holds true for *negative thinking;* in fact, negative thinking power might be even more powerful. Napoleon Hill found out that if you convince yourself of something, there is a higher probability of it happening. He called his effect *"Think and Grow Rich"*. While neither man actually told you what caused these things, there was plenty of evidence of them being true. Abraham Maslow came along with his *"Self-Actualization"* which simply showed that once you become successful, you can begin to help others in a meaningful way. In fact, you have a burning desire to do this. All these people were seeing the same thing that we can call Life Resonance. This won't mean much to you at this time, but everything; I mean everything, is made up of vibrations and there is a "comfortable frequency or resonance" in this vibration.

Let that sink in a second, because this next discussion will be a little weird at first. Life has this same quality and the higher the vibrational resonance, the higher the control over one's environment. Don't put this book down because I said you vibrate. Today we absolutely know that variations in time affect not only how we perceive time but how we interact with reality. In fact; when you travel in a circle at the speed of light, you never grow old. Spin for 10,000 years and stop to find you are still young and vibrant [I am assuming you are vibrant right now as a compliment.] Now spin the other direction for 10,000 years and see what happens. Viola! Oops! You are still vibrant but now all the people you knew died 20 thousand years ago. This relativity thing has to do with our vibrating or spinning "life" and we will look at it a bit so you can attain happiness as we go along.

"Resonance" Changes the Complete Character of things, forces, and life.

Let me give you an example using light. It seems that when light resonates at low frequencies we can see the light in beautiful colors. As its vibration resonance or speed increases we no longer can see this light, but the light beams became more powerful as they turn to X-rays. Even higher frequencies make the light beams able to cut through just about anything as they become cosmic rays. These simple light waves now can damage your cells simply by going through them. The only difference was resonance. If you could change your resonance, you take more control over your environment, but there is a cost and that was hinted to by the words in Matthew, Mark and Luke of the Bible. You begin to lose contact with the carnalness of reality.

We see people changing their resonance every day, but it usually doesn't register nor do we see what it means, but the fairly new science called Participatory Anthropics or Quantum Physics is changing our understanding of what we call reality. If we understand Anthropics we can develop our understanding and control of our environment. To start we must look briefly at something called Quantum Superposition. It's going to be weird, but it helps us understand participative Anthropics which defines how we can actually benefit from the Power of Positive thinking and even how we can move mountains with the faith of a grain of Mustard-seed. Please muddle through this short background.

By the way when those light photons go too slow, they turn into radio waves and if they go slow enough they will miraculously become electricity and shock you. How dumb is this example? These photon things first are sensed by your touch, then hearing, then eyes, then these things go right through you. Someone is telling you this is normal so you believe it and even possibly hold up a sign about how you love photons or some type of mushy thing because you love looking at the physical world so much. I hate to burst a bubble or make you put down a sign, but photons are not really light.

Before I get into our next topic, let me just talk a little bit about how, in school, you were told that photons sometimes were waves with no mass and sometimes they have mass like a really tiny golf ball. They even proved it to you with some crazy experiment and told you that you had better believe it because there was a test on Thursday. Some of the things we will have to talk about are almost as nutty, but there is not test so relax, read and try not to get frustrated when something sounds like photon getting temporary mass. Hopefully, I didn't bring up any bad memories about how stupid you felt thinking matter always had mass, etc. I need to pull you away from the old way of thinking and start getting you to understand that no matter exists except as defined by its vibrating frequency. While that might be hard to sense, I need to pull you away from your comfort zone farther by telling you there are 12 dimensions that control this universe and three of them as associated with something we call cognitive life. Without these three "Cognitive dimensional" qualities, there simply is no reality. All of this is getting us into the realm of Quantum science called participatory Anthropics. Without it there simply is not way to define life and reality. I know you don't believe that right now and some of it sounds nutty, but Einstein, and Niels Bohr relied on Anthropic science to form their theories.

Anthropics in Experimentation

A Physicist named John Archibald Wheeler brought forth the realization of a living, *participatory universe* which was derived from the current Quantum Physics established by Niels Bohr. Here is a quote from Wheeler that may help us here.

Every particle, every field of force, even the space-time continuum itself—derives its function, its meaning, its very existence entirely—even if in some contexts indirectly—from the apparatus-elicited answers to yes-or-no questions, binary choices, bits. That which we call reality arises in the last analysis from the posing of yes-no questions; in short, that all things physical are information-theoretic in origin and that this is a participatory universe.

While the words are weird, he is saying, nothing exists until it is witnessed by a "cognizant viewer" or there are multiple "existences" until witnessed.

This Witness changes the "existence".

The more people "experiencing" events, the more common is the characterization of those events.

The most well-known example of this science is something now known as "Schrodinger's cat". With a cat in a box that also contains poison; the cat is BOTH dead and alive until the box is opened and viewed.

I know that doesn't sound like it has to do with happiness, nor does it help us understand the mysterious verses from the Bible. Before I get back to giving you an answer about the strange verses, let me tell you about some details in experimentation that are well known, but not well understood as they will give some insight.

John Keely was a 19th century genius who never understood his own science of particles. He coined the term for potential matter as being Aether well before Einstein used it to describe dark matter and he understood the finite details inside atoms, but many of his experiments <u>only worked when he was nearby and had a high expectation of success</u>. <u>As he left the room</u>, the results would falter. Finally, he was decried as a charlatan and much of his following left. He went to his grave no knowing why he could not repeat experiments which included levitation systems, an induction resonance motion motor, and many other marvels. In 1872, Keely announced that he discovered a principle for power production based on the vibrations initiated by simple tuning forks. His engine could turn at 800 revolutions per minute and produce 40 hp on less than a thimbleful of water. John is shown with some of his fantastic experiments.

Edward Leedskalnin came along just after John Keely and died in 1951. He, like John, came up with a similar unified field theory that indicated mass really didn't exist, but was established by vibrating magnetism. His Homopolar generator allowed him to levitate 30 ton blocks of coral by himself and build a castle in Florida which he moved to Coral Florida in 1938. While his experiments are documented in a number of patents and a book, no one has been able to recreate what he did every day. The images below show Ed with some of his levitation creations. The middle one shows his generator on top of a lifting structure picking up a massive stone. Without him, the experiments could not be recreated, but there is no doubt that he was successful.

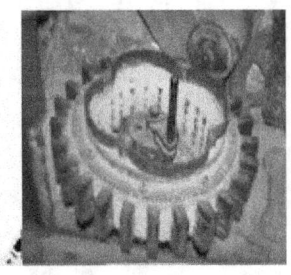

John Hutchison, is the 20th century researcher who is using ultrahigh frequency modulation to perform massive levitation, changing of atomic structures, invisibility and many other seemingly impossible results, is still not sure of how these things happen. <u>He found that he could not repeat similar experiments with the same results</u>. He still has not come to grips with why his experiments were not consistent. While some of the things the Canadian Researcher has accomplished in the last few years are remarkable, let me just show you a couple of the frames from one experiment in the presence of a powerful and strange field of electromagnetic waves. First pliers were picked up and yanked out of the view, but then, a bowling ball rises off the table until the ultrahigh frequency vibrations were halted and the bowling ball resumed its normal heaviness in our reality.

We could spend a long time just going over miraculous experiments and researchers who simply did not recognize how a person could affect an environment.

- Some laugh when they are told about Peter, Elisha, Jesus, and others walked on water because they could not understand how a person can affect his environment.

- Some are in disbelief when they hear that small girls lifting cars off their fathers or loved ones without the girls' ligaments being torn, muscles being ripped, and bones being broken. After dozens of instances, many try to indicate adrenalin keeps the muscles, ligaments, and bones together. They cannot believe people can affect our environment so they believe our body parts become like Iron.

- Some cannot allow themselves to believe the "red shift proof". What I mean by that is according to redshift and detailed calculations; we are in the center of the universe where the Big Bang occurred. Of course that "is" impossible as nothing could have survived the Big Bang explosion. These people also have no understanding of how people affect their environment.

- Many laugh at the Schrodinger Cat story. "It is preposterous that a cat is both dead and alive," they shout, as they have no understanding of how people affect their reality.

- When Einstein was asked if a tree falls in the woods and there is no one around does it make a sound, he simply said, *"There is no tree."* As he understood reality only exists if witnessed by a cognizant entity [meaning us]. He also understood that everyone has an innate genius that is not in our "self" as we are made up of three entities that I am going to introduce right now.

Everyone is a genius. But if you judge a fish on its ability to climb a tree, it will live its whole life believing that it is stupid.

Here is one of his sage sayings and it has something to do with our subject. One cannot be truly happy if he or she is focusing on the wrong things. With that, let's start out by defining what a person is and what God is. If you remember form the Genesis story, we were made in the image of God. What in the world does that mean?

Self, Soul, Spirit

If you have ever wondered why in the Christian religion, God is three entities in one, or if you are one of those who thinks it is absurd that the Creator has three "persons"; quit it right now.

Sumerian	They had a Trinity-Enki, Kisar, and Nudimmud
Maori	They believed that three Gods made man. They also had the belief that woman came from man's rib.
Celtic	Hoa, Hea, and Hu make up the creator trinity
Peru	Tanga the creator was one God –in-three
Persia	Ormuzid, Mithras, and Ahriman made up the holy trinity
Syria	Monimus, Aziz, and Ares were the creator trinity
Canaanites	Baal was called the self-triplicating god
Hittites	Sius, Tiwaz, and Taru made the trinity
China –Tao and Buddha	The God Trinity controls the world according to their ancient custom.
Egypt	Trinity-Mut, Khonsu, and AmonRa made up their trinity.
Greek	The Greeks had their trinity as well- Zeus, Hades, and Cronus
Norse	The Trinity of gods, Odin, Vili, and Ve, controlled everything according to tradition.
Hindu	Hindu Trinity was made up of Vishnu, Brahma,& Siva.
Ancient India	Varuna, Dyaus, and Paranjayas made the trinity.
Jewish, Christian	Jewish and Christian belief is that the Trinity is individualized as Lord God, Jesus, and Holy Ghost.
Etruscan	The Etruscan Trinity is Tinin, Menrva, and Uni.
Akkadim	The Trinity for the Akkadim were Ellil, Ea, and Anu
Ethiopia	Even Ethiopia had a Trinity- Beher, Astar, and Mahrem.
Urantia	The mystical work of the Urantia calls out the trinity as Khaldi, Theispas, and Artinis.
Palmyrene [ancient Syria]	The Trinity to the ancient Syrians was Yarhibol, Bel, and Aglibol.
Bantu tribe Africa	The creator God was really three [Nzame, Mebere, and Nkwa].
Slavs	Svarog, Svantovit, and Perun made the trinity.
Baltics	Suaxtix, Dievs, and Perkunas made the trinity.

The previous chart shows that almost all ancient historical records defining the creator in any religion defines "him" a TRIUNE. We, just like our creator, are three entities in one. We are told over and over and new science is allowing us to understand just what that means. While certainly a limited description, the three entities of God may be identified below. Hopefully the drawing below helps show how a Triune creator can be depicted

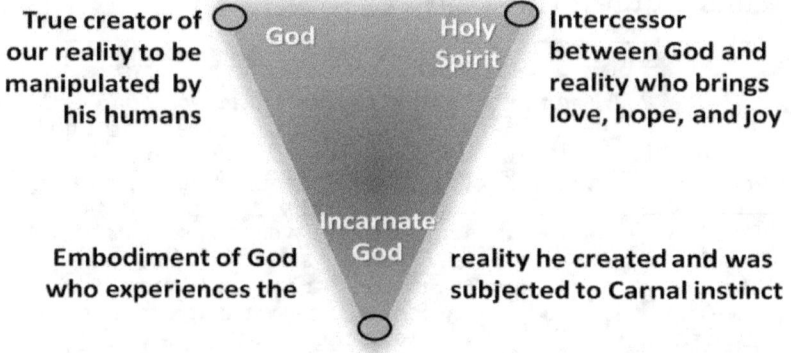

We will see that not only is this three entities in one needed for our interpretation of creator, but also that it was NOT crazy for God incarnate to talk to the Creator God in the New Testament stories. Have you ever "known" that you should or should not do something, by some instinct or, whatever? Then; there you were doing what you KNEW to be wrong? For a while the "don't do it you" was winning but the "go ahead and do it" pushed the other one away. Don't even try to tell me you have never had that problem. We see it every day. Some sexual encounter that no sane person would ever do, but ---BAM!--- the other entity inside pushed forth and caused some horrible disaster. The Creator and God

Incarnate had similar discussions but unlike us, Jesus listened to the other him.

God's Image

We are told humans are made in God's image. Our being is not simply DNA expanding to make skin and veins. Instead our being is characterized by 3 mutually perpendicular vibrationally established, dimensional elements that help establish what we call reality. I'm sure you have an idea about these, but here is a simple description.

"Self"- This is the part that <u>participates in reality</u> and is filled with instincts of lust, envy, fear of survival, etc. This is <u>the brain driven part</u>. While many try to tell you the brain creates our reality from vibrational inputs through the eyes, nose, tongue, ears, and fingers, the brain only builds up synaptic bridges of sensations and memories and acts on these memories in accordance with DNA makeup. For instance, the brain may like the sensation of smell of a nearby female which triggers desire. The taste of a food which triggers comfort, the sight of recreated images it witnesses triggering a warm feeling, or the touch of something warm which triggers a muscle reflex, but it is a long way from "Reality". Certainly, our brain stores memories established by sensation and recreation of reality, but it has no control over that reality. Even with its horrible limitations, it is the part of us we try to protect as it is our direct interface with reality. <u>This part dies</u> after a time.

"Soul"- This is the <u>most important part of you</u>. Sometimes called "id" or <u>subconscious</u> it is the part that

23

helps define our reality. It establishes answers outside our base feelings and calculations to provide us a broader understanding of life. It establishes how we relate outside our vision of self and is the part of us that imparts empathy. The soul never dies, but instead it can allow for us to gain a new "self" on occasion. Because our soul never dies, this is the part of us that will finally end up with a new life in our linked universe [Heaven] or will drift without a reality for all eternity after the end of this reality we see, feel, and hear today. The thing that makes this important to this discussion is that the soul can manipulate or change what we normally define as reality if our focus is on this part of our lives. On the downside, the soul cannot exactly experience reality without the "self" portion of life.

"Spirit"- This portion provides a link between this universe and our linked universe. We can think of it as similar to a black hole that allows matter to move between universes, but, in this case, we are talking about communication between God and man to guide us. As shown next this portion of our being supplies our wisdom, true love, and faith in God. As far as happiness goes, this part is very important as well as it allows us to understand love and happiness even when horrible things happen to us and those around us. A simple diagram of us as a three dimensionally characterized entity is given next. Please do not worry that it is incomplete.

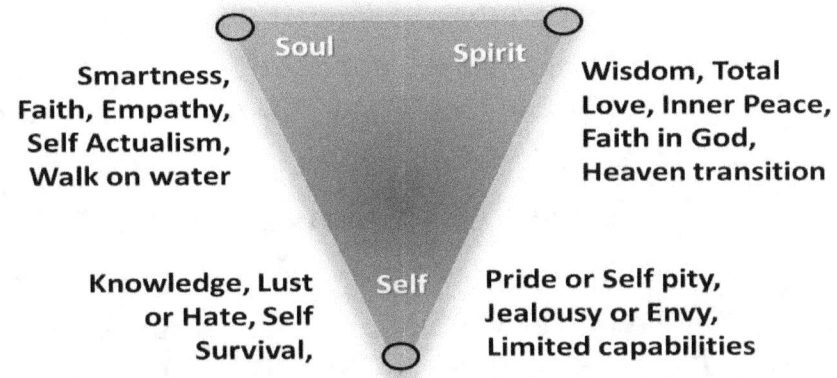

With all that, maybe we can get a rough understand of the three Bible verses I introduced earlier and begin to understand what the meaning has for true happiness.

Let me try to paraphrase the three Bible verses I brought up before.

- *God Incarnate said if you want your "soul portion of life" to thrive", don't worry about your "the self or carnal life".*

- *He reiterated his command a second time indicating that if one <u>focuses</u> on success in this reality, he will lower the ability of his soul to control his environment.*

- *He reiterated it a third time saying there is nothing that we have as precious as our living soul.*

- *He reiterated it a 4th time saying some of the souls- of his followers will be reanimated in some way and still be alive [and conscious] when he returns in very few years.*

- *He emphasized a 5th time by having the living souls of Elijah and Moses come back into a human-like appearance to show these guys that their souls could not die."*

What a Contradiction!

Please notice that life and soul are sometimes interchangeable this is why he said saving your life loses your life. The second life is the life of the SOUL [most important part of you]. Let me give some more detail from John.

John 6:65-- ----*The <u>Spirit gives life [Soul]; the flesh [self] counts for nothing</u>.*

Taoist-The Bible is only one place; the Taoists said it this way.

- *For happiness, think lightly of yourself and deeply of the world.*

- *<u>Doing nothing is better than being busy doing nothing.</u>*

- *Cut doors and windows for a room; <u>it is the holes which make it useful.</u> Happiness is like a window.*

- *For happiness think of your life as an empty vessel.*

Happiness is like a window

Buddhists defined Chakra levels that would separate you from the carnal world to bring happiness. Chakras are advanced by changing one's vibrational resonance.

Frequencies

26

Whether you already know about the new descriptions of Matter, Force, and Life in the vibrational world or not are not the main targets for this book but possibly, a little insight into photonics and matter would be useful.

Common Material Frequencies

Let me start by saying; today quantum physicists will tell you there is no such thing as matter. Like the "Light" example I provided, the complexity of matter is determined by how fast "potential matter" [AETHER] vibrates gold vibrates faster than helium, for instance. The following tables show you actual and/or theoretical frequency and wavelength standards of common elements known today along with other attributes of other characteristics of our universe. The material frequencies have been derived from the various groups investigating vibration reaction of structures/atoms. How would you like some particles vibrating at 60 exahertz? That vibration causes Gold, as you can see from the list following. Have the right frequency or resonate the environment around a substance and one can make ANY material you want. Notice that most frequencies do not form matter, at least structures with mass. Even the smallest physical component [BOSON] must vibrate fairly fast [300 MHz] so one would think that if you wanted to modify particles, you had better have a source that can vibrate very, very fast. One thing to note as you look at the tables; vibrating frequencies that create the element we call Meitnerium can even vibrate faster to produce the limits of matter to what we call pure magnetism. Some call it a black hole. It is known that the event horizon of a black hole can take dark matter and convert it into much higher frequency "visible matter" and we find that we can do the same thing if we resonate at a high enough frequency.

Chart of Particle Vibrations

Name or characteristic	Maximum Wavelength [meters]	Highest Frequency [Hertz]
Aether [??]	$*1 \times 10^{+10}$	$<30 \times 10^{-3}$
Fermion [part mass]	$*1 \times 10^{+4}$	30×10^3
Boson [smallest mass]	$*1 \times 10^{-0}$	30×10^7
Baryon [electron]	$*1 \times 10^{-3}$	30×10^{10}
Hydrogen/1	1×10^{-9}	30×10^{16}
Berylium/9	1×10^{-10}	30×10^{17}
Silicon/28	3.5×10^{-11}	8.5×10^{18}
Zirconium/91	1×10^{-11}	30×10^{18}
Gold/197	5×10^{-12}	60×10^{18}
Meitnerium/270	3.7×10^{-12}	27×10^{19}
Straight Gravity	smaller	higher

This table represents the form of the structural dimensions that we use in our reality. To keep matter operational in our universe we also have force vibrations called Electro-magnetics. The vibrational levels for these waves are well known and shown below:

Chart of Electro-Magnetic Vibrations

Name or characteristic	Maximum Wavelength [meters]	Highest Frequency [Hertz]
Electricity	5×10^{10}	$<30 \times 10^{-3}$
Brain function	5×10^{7}	6×10^{0} to 10^{1}
Human hearing	1×10^{4}	20×10^{3}
VHF [radio]	1×10^{0}	30×10^{7}
UHF [radio]	1×10^{-1}	30×10^{8}
SHF [radio]	1×10^{-2}	30×10^{9}
EHF [radio]	1×10^{-3}	30×10^{10}
Microwaves	2.5×10^{-4}	12×10^{12}
Infrared [light]	1×10^{-6}	30×10^{13}
Visible light	4×10^{-7}	75×10^{13}
X-rays	1×10^{-8}	30×10^{15}
Gamma Rays	1×10^{-9}	30×10^{16}
Magnetism	lower	higher

The thing we know about electromagnetic frequencies is that less input energy is required for a particular action the higher the frequency of the action. It becomes easier to attain a purer, higher quality resonance and the force becomes greater until it is pure magnetism. We can model life the same way and look at the next chart.

Chart of Life Function

Name or characteristic	Maximum Wavelength [meters]	Highest Frequency [Hertz]
Molecular Interaction	5×10^{10}	$<30 \times 10^{-3}$
Unaware Life	1×10^4	30×10^3
Life Awareness	1×10^0	30×10^7
Survival	1×10^{-3}	30×10^{10}
Sex	1×10^{-9}	30×10^{16}
Need for Companionship	1×10^{-10}	30×10^{17}
Need to help others [Self Actualized]	3.5×10^{-11}	8.5×10^{18}
Selfless Love	5×10^{-12}	60×10^{18}
Universal Understanding	3.7×10^{-12}	27×10^{19}
Insight into the External World	smaller	Higher

I know this list sounds completely foreign to you right now and they look more like a pictorial reference of some Buddhist monk, but please stay with me as we will find as we head through Anthropic Science that how one "realizes" his existence actually changes his existence and the existence of those around him. As you may already be aware, there is something to "Think and Grow Rich" and "Self-Actualization", you have read about. According to Norman Vincent Peale's "positive thinking", as positive thinking is more in control, happiness increases. There are many studies. Right now, just check out the previous chart showing self-actualization, selfless love, and universal understanding. Once you know how to do it, simply increasing what we can call life force frequency, life has more meaning and happiness ensues. We are not just talking about happiness here. No matter how you sense it, increasing your vibrational resonance frequency also increases your power over your environment. At the very high frequencies, there is almost no need for the environment. If you read the Bible it was best said by Jesus. *With faith the size of a grain of mustard-seed, one can tell mountains to move---and they will.* I don't think you will be doing that right away, but the point Jesus was making is that you can begin to control you entire reality simply by doing what he said three time and I listed before.

Luke 9:23-*For* <u>whoever wants to save their life will lose it</u>*, but whoever loses their life for me will save it.*

Paraphrased-*If you want to truly experience life, you must separate yourself from this reality sufficiently.* Now the part about do this for Jesus will allow you to save your life is an important part as well, but well beyond the limitations of this book as it deals with life after life.

How Is this Interpreted in the Previous Chart?

Eliminating the lower frequency elements [selfish desire, instinct for sex, and fear for survival] allows you to sustain the higher levels longer and better. The key to happiness, we will find is obtaining these high frequencies. Hopefully, I can help you understand how to get to these levels.

Beat frequencies of Life

One of the truths of "Positive Thinking" is this. If 2 people get together and somehow one increases his frequency, by love, empathy, motivational conquest, disregarding personal survival, or altruistic thinking; just being near another will make the frequencies of the second person higher. He will feel better. As he feels better, the first person also gains. If, on the other hand, a depressed person comes near, you will probably feel a little worse than normal. There have been hundreds of experiments on this theme and all are spooky. People can solve problems faster if many people are trying to solve the problem *EVEN IF THEY ARE NOT COMMUNICATING WITH EACH OTHER*. Think of it the way radio works. If a singer has a 1 Khz tone to be transmitted on a radio station channel at 454 KHz, the 2 are added together to make 455KHz as the frequency of the entire radio signal is increased. This is called the positive Beat Frequency. And listening to a 454 KHz channel we can hear the 1 KHz that was added. Unfortunately there is a negative side.

Bad Beat Frequencies

This whole "*get in a group trying to expand awareness*" thing has just as bad of an effect. If a mob builds and lowers the consciousness frequencies with debased attitudes [Hate, Lust, Survival, etc.], the entire group

'Vibration" will be lowered *EVEN IF THERE IS NO VERBAL CONTACT BETWEEN EACH OF THE MOB MEMBERS*. This has been proven over and over again. This is because beat frequencies go both ways. A 1 KHz signal and a 454 KHz signal ALSO make a 453 KHz "SUBTRACTED" frequency. We see the beat frequencies in electro-magnetics all the time and we can easily sense beat frequencies of sound pressure. Believe me when I tell you, the same happens with consciousness.

Get with the wrong people and you can greatly limit any greatness you can have. Get near the right people and your world will be opened up. It's not magic it vibrations and resonance.

Hopefully, you are beginning to realize your life is much more than simply a calculating brain that has blood pumped into it to take part in sensing our reality.

Realizations

We must consider life differently than we used to. The universe without life might not exist. For us, we can certainly say it would not exist because we would not exist. Life is not DNA so don't go thinking it's covered by a volume of particles. Interestingly live and dead DNA look the same.

How about our consciousness? Does our sub consciousness exist? If it does exist the question might be "If I had no subconsciousness, would the universe cease to exist?" Some will say that people being here or not being here have no effect on the world at all. This is not correct and there is something we do know. This "sub consciousness thing" [Soul] is not governed by the 4 normal dimensions. Therefore, we need to investigate how it is constructed in this universe.

What about LIFE itself? The question would be, "If there were no life, would the universe exist?" Some may just say, "Who cares?", but Anthropic Science says; *nothing exists in this reality* is no cognizant viewer is present.

Does reality exist? The simple answer is NO, but there is a lot more to it. We cannot communicate with each *other without a reality and without a large number of entities holding this reality together; the concept of light would melt away so let's not dwell on this one as we have people all over the place.*

How does the "Soul" portion and "Self" portion work in our lives? A possible beginning to this answer is something I made up years ago concerning what people go into what jobs. As you can see from the following chart the people predominantly trying to use knowledge as a basis for life tend to reduce the suggestions and understanding of their soul and rely more on the awareness of their brain itself.

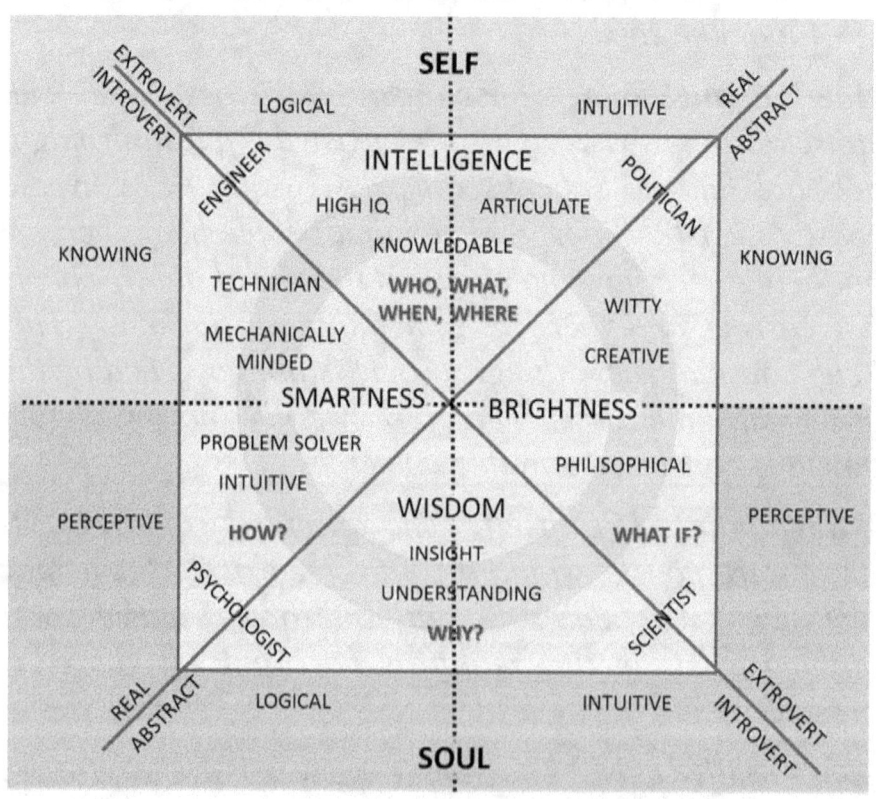

36

Those who channel wisdom, do it by opening up their consciousness to understandings beyond self. These are the people who listen to that small voice going against what feels good. From the chart we can see that the person gains insight, understanding, perception, intuition, and becomes more philosophical no matter if they are introverted or extraverted, or if their brains deal more with real or abstract concepts.

We will see that this type of <u>push to gain wisdom</u> will eventually allow for true happiness, while the miserable seeking scientist or engineer boxes his appreciation of our world into known criteria.

In simple terms do not rely on what your brain can do if you want expanded understanding, free flowing wisdom, and true happiness.   Let me give you a little more information about all three entities that make you. Don't worry that the Egyptians called then the Shadow, the KAA, and the BAA and Freud called them the ID, EGO, and super-ego. We will use the Biblical description and compare them later. Well, let me at least separate knowledge from wisdom for you. The best place to find out about wisdom is from a wise man named Solomon. If you don't like the Bible parts in this book, just think Freud or another said these things.

Proverbs 24:3-4 *By wisdom a house is built, and through understanding it is established; through knowledge its rooms are filled with rare and beautiful treasures. [The understanding of needing the house is entirely different that the knowledge that was used to get playthings that have no worth.].*

Proverbs 8:11 *For wisdom is more precious than rubies, and nothing you desire can compare with her. [Wisdom is more important the knowledge that can bring you wealth.]*

Proverbs 19:8 *He who gets wisdom loves his own soul; he who cherishes understanding prospers. [This is the same, but it directs us to the soul part of our being as the imparter of wisdom.]*

Proverbs 13:20 *He who walks with the wise grows wise, but a companion of fools suffers harm. [Same, same, same]*

Proverbs 24:5-6 *A wise man has great power, and a man of knowledge increases strength. For waging war you need guidance, and for victory many advisers. [In this case the war is won by wisdom.]*

Genesis 2:17 *But you must not eat from the tree of the knowledge of good and* evil, *for when you eat of it you will surely die. [Have you ever wondered why God would not want humans knowledgeable??? I could tell you but then you won't have to read my book.]*

Proverbs 3:5,7a *Trust in the Lord with all your heart, and lean not on your own understanding.... Do not be wise in your own eyes. [Wise in your own eyes is not wisdom, if you didn't already know it.]*

I'm sorry I got a little carried away in the Bible stuff, but there is so much science nested in that book that I marvel at its simplicity and complexity. I'll try not to go overboard as we continue and start getting into just who you really are. If you know who you are, you have a

38

better chance at being truly happy. By the way, leaning out you own understanding and partaking of the fruit of the tree of knowledge and prospering from you own understanding is not the way to happiness.

Life Group

As I mentioned before our universe apparently has 12 dimensions rather than the 4 you were taught in school years ago. There dimensions deal with manufacturing what appears for be matter [particles, gravity and black holes], 3 dimensions deal with manufacturing what appears we call forces [electricity, magnetism, light, etc.], 3 dimensions deal with manufacturing what we call time, and 3 dimensions produce what we call life and more importantly cognizant viewers. As each of the 3 components of life MUST be part of our reality or our reality cannot be [according to Anthropic science, Quantum superposition, etc.], the characteristics of our being are truly dimensional elements of the universe, so let's describe them that way.

Self-Dimension –

This is what people see. It is your carnal character, sexual interest and attraction, physical self, body, pride, hunger, vanity, smartness, the almost unnatural feeling for self-preservation, and the awareness that you alive.

DNA chemical modifications and optical transmission are part of this "Dimension". These are all parts of what we can call the SELF. These all make up a veneer that interacts with others in a physical way. We have no real scientific group trying to define the life energy, but let me give it a try, knowing the similarities of the other 2 dimensional elements of our universe. Electricity [potential Photonic Energy] and Aether [potential for matter] dimensions have a similarity to SELF [potential for cognizant life]. "Self" resides in what we call reality as soon as it begins to vibrate. *Some call this the Consciousness or the conscious mind, but most of the time it is exactly the opposite and it is totally consumed by instinct.* It is controlled by chemical stimuli as multiple synaptic bridges connect chemical/vibrational memories. It honors things like Orgasm, full stomach, warm blanket, and seeing a cute smile erupt on your face. It turns from glad to mad in an instant when a driver cuts you off accidentally. It is the dimension that experiences reality as we normally view it. "Self" itself [try putting that in a sentence!] is made up of vibrating chemical responses set to some generally unknown master clock. It isn't the proteins of DNA that are life it is this vibration thing partially caused by electrical transfer of one Chromosome to another. No matter what we do to remove this control from our true selves, the Self keeps popping back to hinder our push to true happiness. I will concede that most indicate this is the conscious mind and people are awake for this instinct brain to work. There also is a calculating brain to consider and a memory brain to contend with so

41

consciousness really has many levels. As I indicated before, all the memorizing and knowledge one can accumulate and recall with this part of our life force will not lead us to true happiness. We need to strive for wisdom.

Subconscious or Soul Dimension

The soul is a characterization of the kinetic or vibrating self. The subconscious is not life but its vibrational essence "lives" perpendicular to life. Some call this dimension the Soul of a person, or the ID. Some define this as the little voice in the back of your head or premonition or self-actualization characterization. This is going to sound weird, but think of this as a cause and effect because "the subconscious" reacts with "vibrations of life" like "magnetism" reacts to vibrating "electricity", or like gravity reacts to vibrations of matter. By affecting the vibrational level, "life" is changed and visa-versa. If a life vibration is halted, the subconscious must find another life to be able to sustain itself in this universe. I know I went spooky on you for a moment, but as you read this book please understand, I am not trying to devise a result. I'm simply trying to look at the stresses on the universe that make what we call reality so we can understand and gain more happiness.

The soul is the real you.

It reacts with and can sometimes modify how we perceive, sense and combine realities. The neat thing about this "part" of you is <u>it doesn't die</u> like the "SELF".

42

It is the part that desperately love's everyone and wants to help them. If there was one reason Adam was not to eat that knowledge fruit it was that it stifles this part of the YOU. Let me quickly touch on something that is fairly new in human biologic studies and that is our secondary brain. It seems the Heart has a fairly large cluster of neurons that senses love, remembers feelings and something very strange, it transmits RF messages much more vigorously than our massive heat brain. For this study, it makes no difference. I just thought that if you had heard the phrase I love you with all my heart, now you know it is not just an arbitrary meaningless message. That brings us to the weirdest part of life called the soul. Egyptians called it the Baa.

Spirit Dimension

The "spirit" can be considered as a glow. It is a window between this world and beyond. The part of us survives beyond reality. The diagram following is one I typically use to show you an initial impression of our three entities. While the subconscious is somewhat difficult to grasp initially, this "spirit" dimensional quality is even more difficult, but just as important to our universe as it becomes the Self-soul force just like the dual of electro-magnetic force. Similar to pure magnetism-force or pure gravity-matter [black hole], this element or spirit-life can barrel its way to our linked universe just like a black hole is a gateway for matter. We won't discuss much about this part of life too much as it is beyond this topic.

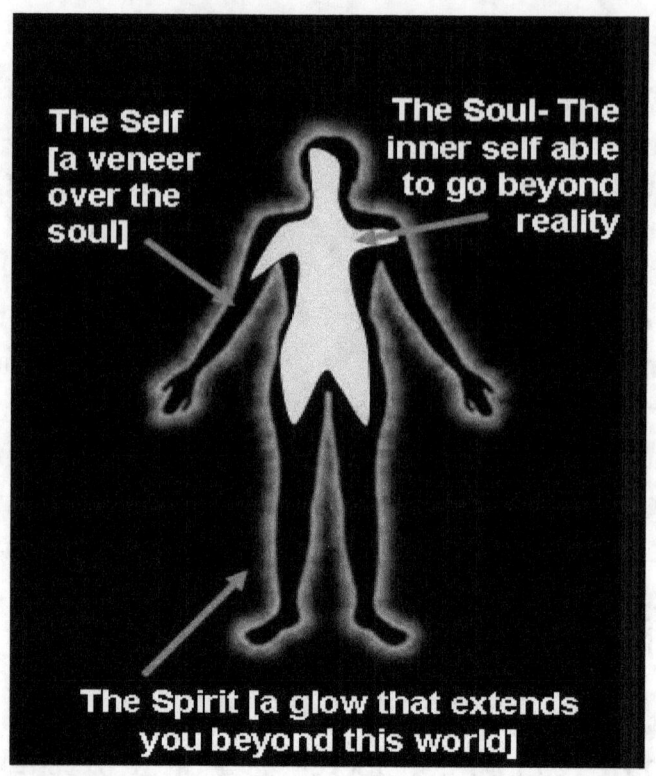

The Self [a veneer over the soul]

The Soul- The inner self able to go beyond reality

The Spirit [a glow that extends you beyond this world]

The answer to what our life dimensions are isn't simple, nor can the dimensions be defined in a simple image, but hopefully you are gaining enough insight to allow you to understand the soul part a little more as this will help us gain happiness. With that I'm going back to the Bible, but we could find these insights in many ancient religious works.

1. *The Bible says dust to dust when referring to the self or body. When our body dies, it is no more. Don't go thinking that is the end, but when you are renewed, you will be different. You self will be brand new.*

2. The Bible says, our soul can live or die after we die. This will be described in more detail as we go along.

The warning is this- *"What profits a man who gains much but loses his soul?"*

3. <u>The Bible indicates that your soul may have several bodies</u> before our spirit is released. Reincarnated souls are described in the Bible and many other ancient texts around the world.

No doubt about it; like most religions, the entire Christian religion is molded around the fact that the SOUL dimension of life is many times more important than the "Self" portion. Like Christianity, most religions identify the soul as the real entity of man. I think Taoist say it best by telling the followers that if they are to be happy, they must think of themselves [the self-entity] as an empty vessel. The Bible teaches the same thing it just says it in a slightly different way.

"If you want to live, you must die"

This isn't dying in the way we normally think of it. What the book tries to tell us is that if we try to enhance our Carnal SELF, we will lose our much more important SOUL. Losing your soul is a true death, so let's not let that happen. There is no true happiness in that.

I think I need to stop explaining and just get to examples and ancient textual verification on most of the elements of life as a controlling element of our reality. All I can tell you for sure is that the universe doesn't exist without life and the more aware a being is of its life, the higher would be its vibrational frequency. For instance, bacteria would be a low frequency while humans would be represented by a much higher frequency and life-energy.

45

To try to understand life [the dimensions of life] let's look at some of the ancient texts and see if we can glean information that will be useful to us. I have selected a small sampling from the ancient Gnostics, and Essene to help out here. Both of these groups tried to understand the extremely ancient texts of their day. The Essene tried their best to write down the exact meanings of the ancient words, while the Gnostics tried to put the details into a story so that the words could be understood better. Our first stop is to the "Book of Giants".

"Book of Giants"

As you might guess, this book is about ancient giants that ruled over mankind many thousands of years ago. It was written <u>well before</u> much of the Bible. From the Book of Giants [a number of copies were found as part of the 'Essene's" Dead Sea Scrolls] we read about angels who came from another universe [heaven] to help mankind. Don't be worried about someone talking about angels. The word is actually "watchers" and the Egyptians and Hebrews both talked about these interesting "watchers". By the time of this *Book of Giants*" story, many watchers had been turned back into humans called the Anak. Egyptians called them the Lords of Amenti and the Sumerians called them Anunnaki. Unfortunately, the same old story we have heard a hundred times happened during this ancient time. The Anak people sort of began to think of themselves as Gods and let's see what happened.

For they [The Anak people from the Pleistocene Age.] *knew the secrets of heaven. Sin was great in the Earth because of their experiments. They made mistakes and they killed many animals and people.* [What we see is that these "knowledgeable people" tried to make or modify life itself. This ended up killing a bunch of people and animals. I know we are doing the same thing today, but let's continue.]

They were "with" women and they begat giants. [If you can't change something one way there is always sex.]

They selected two hundred donkeys, two hundred asses, two hundred rams of the flock, two hundred goats, two hundred other beasts of the field. From every animal, and from every type of human was taken its seed for mixed sex. After a time they defiled the animals and people and begot giants, monsters, and dragons. God saw all that they begot, and, behold, all the Earth was corrupted with their blood and by the hand of man. [I think you can see that these giants weren't creating ANY life, they were simply mixing DNA to bastardize God's creativity in making LIFE.]

They were brought food which did not suffice for them and they turned on mankind. They began to hunger and they were seeking to devour many animals and people. The people ran to a safe place but the monsters and dragons attacked it. Man's flesh was eaten by all the giants, monsters, and dragons. The monsters thought that they would be saved and they would arise after death, but it was not so because they were lacking in true knowledge of heaven and because they were of the Earth. They grew corrupt and did not worship the almighty God. They were considering separation of Giants from the angels upon the Earth, but to no avail. In the end they perished and died because they caused great corruption in the Earth and because they tormented the Earth. [Suffice to say they were tormented after death.]

What we find is really smart humans living during very ancient times. While they were smart, they didn't know what life was. These people were creating all types of animals at this ancient time. [I know you are struggling with this, but just go with it as it won't hurt.] The Bible called the animals "Unclean or abominations" and we are just now relearning how to do similar types of animal creations. There is no doubt that the ancient geneticists were more knowledgeable about life, but they still had NO IDEA what it was. Let's read further. The reason this is important to this discussion is that these people abandoned their "souls" for knowledge. This time we will read again from another one of the Dead Sea Scrolls.

"Book of Secrets"

To give you a feeling of how different life is than DNA we have to bring up the "Book of Secrets". The "Book of Secrets" found with the Dead Sea Scrolls provides a strong warning about the use of "secrets of God". The book simply says that if we try to misuse the secrets of life, the same thing will happen to mankind that had happened before. The earth would be destroyed again. This destruction would not be by direct intervention of God, but because we, as humans, don't understand what we are doing as we manipulate "Nature". Of the secret elements indicated in the text, it seems that the "manipulation of creation" or trying to create life is the worst. This probably references the genetic manipulation and transmutation or one material into another [Alchemy]. By all accounts, the Ancient people living during the time of Adam employed both of these things before and immediately after the worldwide flood at the end of the Pleistocene Age. Here are the major elements of what has been pieced together of the "Book of Secrets"; judge for yourself.

If it makes you fearful, you read it correctly.

Those who would penetrate the origins of knowledge, along with those who hold fast to the wonderful mysteries of magic; --Those who walk in simplicity as well as those who are devious in every activity of the deeds of humanity; those with a stiff neck, and all the mass of the Gentiles, [Gentiles were all people who were not considered "Chosen Ones" like the Jews and other pure descendants from Noah.]

--With this I beseech your attention. All of the secrets of sin and magic were known but they [The humans living in the Pleistocene, including the Anak people] *did not know the secret of the way things are nor did they understand the things of old.* [They didn't understand what LIFE really was. We can imagine they didn't even consider their soul as they pushed harder and harder into a KNOWLEDGE based world.]

They did not know what would come upon them, so they did not rescue themselves <u>without the secret of the way things are. -- It is not a human possession to act on wisdom.</u> It is not possible because wisdom is hidden except for the wisdom of cunning evil, and the schemes of Belial [One of these Anak People] who modified creation, a thing that ought never to be done again, except by the command of his Maker. [This is the important part coming up]. <u>*Only God has the wisdom to modify creation.*</u> *Belial* [Anak] *modified creation and it should NEVER be done again.* [While this includes genetic manipulation it seems to include manipulation of matter as well.]

Consider the soothsayers, those teachers of sin and magic. Do not regard your foolishness, for the <u>vision is sealed up from you, and you have not properly understood the eternal mysteries.</u> [Just in case you

51

didn't get it the first time, it is stated again. Manipulation of nature cannot be understood by man. It is foolish to try to use these things for good. I know we are using genetic engineering today to help many things, but this is saying the apparent help will not last and it will not bring happiness.]

Finally the Real Issue

You have not become wise in understanding my secrets; for you have not properly understood the origin of Wisdom.

Everything accomplished without WISDOM is a fool's work. No matter how great one becomes, <u>he will suffer because he used his own intelligence to establish what he thought was greatness</u>. Happiness will elude him and he will not be comforted by his greatness.

The truth in the "Book of Secrets" is to strive for wisdom. Wisdom is only obtained from the part of you that cannot die---your soul. Listen, learn, understand, and separate yourself from knowledge gained by your "SELF". Then you can gain TRUE HAPPINESS.

Don't be thinking these 2 books only address actions before the Pleistocene Extinction. They are still relevant today. So if we want to limit the control of our "Self" portion and increase control of our "Soul" portion; how can it be done?

Gaining wisdom increases true Happiness. Wisdom comes when we are separated from the "self".

52

Removing Self

If matter cannot be created or destroyed, we can assume that LIFE has the same characteristic. I can tell that I'm losing you. You're thinking that when someone dies, life must be lost, but life may be reborn somewhere else. You are thinking that the number of people continuously increases over time, but in fact, if we look at the people living on the earth during the Pleistocene from Adam on, we would find that there have been many population peaks over the ages with just as many people as we find in the world today.

Killed off by war, famine, disease, and age, human Life may even be recycled so to speak. That does not mean that a person becomes a bug in our next life, so don't worry that you stepped on grandma. It does absolutely mean this outer skin is not the important part of life nor is it the part you need to feed to gain happiness.

What Not to Do

Every time you satisfy a lustful desire, or a hunger for 20 hamburgers, or get your hair curled to impress someone, or delay some work to simply relax; you are <u>sinking farther and farther **FROM** happiness</u>. The first time you get mad at something someone received, or flare up when someone gets something you thought you deserved; when someone cuts you off on the highway and you get angry or someone "hurts you feelings" you are also forcing happiness away. If someone answers a question wrong and you correct him to show you know more than he; or even if someone hurts you and you don't immediately forgive his actions and try to help him over his anger; your SELF is taking control and your vibrational resonance, so to speak, is lowered making you less aware of and giving you less control over your REALITY. These things also make it more difficult for you to help those around you which is one thing that can be done to enhance awareness and happiness.

When Abraham Maslow suggested that only someone successful can become self- actualized to allow him to have the empathy for others to change the environment, he did not mean success at money, power, position or fame. The way to gain empathy is to reduce or, if possible eliminate feelings and actions of SELF. This self-actualization not only opens our being to help others, it also increases our innate vibrational resonance.

Modifications of this vibration, changes the characteristics of life itself. It can become more dynamic or less expansive. Higher frequency vibration components may live longer or the life function may be enhanced. This means to always strive to eliminate SELF in all that you do, think, say, dream, or feel. Don't get me wrong. Just as you think you are beginning to love everyone, some good looking girl with a nice look butt comes by and you will have to start all over. While you want to think about something else, your "Self" is the part that is drawn in by the object of stored fat on a woman. The desire and mood make absolutely no sense, but self can be characterized as ***internalization of reality*** and easily recognized as sensations of self, survival, and sex. Do not be upset that you failed; just continue working on it. Let me bring in Bible stuff again as I think it explains this pretty well.

Romans 3:10-18 - *"None is righteous* [able to separate from "self"]*, no, not one; no one understands; no one seeks for God. All have turned aside; together they have become worthless; no one does good, not even one. Their throat is an open grave; they use their tongues to deceive. The venom of asps is under their lips. Their mouth is full of curses and bitterness."* [No matter how hard you try you will not be able to keep Self, Sex, and survival from creeping back into your life.]

Romans 7:13-24- *I* [This is talking about Paul the Apostle] *am unspiritual, sold as a slave to sin* [Sin is a code word for carnal nature]. *I do not understand what I do. For what I want to do I do not do, but what I hate I do. And if I do what I do not want to do, -- As it is, it is no longer I myself who do it, but it is sin living in me. For I know that good itself does not dwell in me, that is, in my sinful nature. For I have the desire to do what is good, but I cannot carry it out. For I do not do the good I want to do, but the evil I do not want to do—this I keep on doing. Now if I do what I do not want to do, it is no*

longer I who do it, but it is sin living in me that does it.--
What a wretched man I am! [Please understand Paul was
a holy man who was almost killed a number of times
and finally beheaded in his attempt to cast away self to
honor God and he failed many times.]

Romans 8:13 *For if you live according to the flesh, you
will die; but if by the Spirit you put to death the
misdeeds of the body, you will live.* [If this sounds
familiar it should. Over and over the New Testament
recites this thing to help you understand how to gain true
happiness by moving away from the Carnal "Reality"
we are driven back to continuously.]

I know you are thinking I'm saying it is useless to try to
gain happiness as we can never escape this self-
aggrandizing part of life wallowing in our conceited or
self-importance façade being drawn to gratifications of
sex, gluttony, and other things. Soon someone wrote
them down.

What are Self Problems?

The book of "Proverbs" has something called the 7
carnal sins and the book of "Galatians" has something
called the sins of the flesh, and later these were
compiled as the 7 deadly sins. These really describe the
self. While they don't seem bad, what these things do is
weaken control of the most important part of life which
we call the soul. Here is the description of self.

Proverbs 6:16-19- *These six things doth the LORD hate:
yea, seven are an abomination unto him:*

- **Pride** *[in yourself]*
- *Lying [to protect self]*
- *Killing[to protect self]*
- *Wicked imagining*
- *Making mischief*
- *False witness*

Many of these don't seem like horrible things, but they drive us into having "self" control" us rather than the soul centered life to gain true happiness.

Galatians 5:19-21-Now the works of the flesh are evident, which are:

- *Fornication/sex,*
- *lewdness,*
- *Idolatry/sorcery*
- *Hatred*
- *Envy/ jealousies,*
- *selfish ambition,*
- *murder,*
- *drunkenness*

Like the first set, indicated, we control our universe with our soul, <u>we satisfy our self by ignoring the soul</u>.

Later Compilation

These were all, sort of compiled into a single theme as indicated below:

- gluttony
- lust
- greed
- pride
- **<u>Sorrow</u>**
- hatred
- vanity
- laziness

Some examples of the ways to eliminate happiness are shown next.

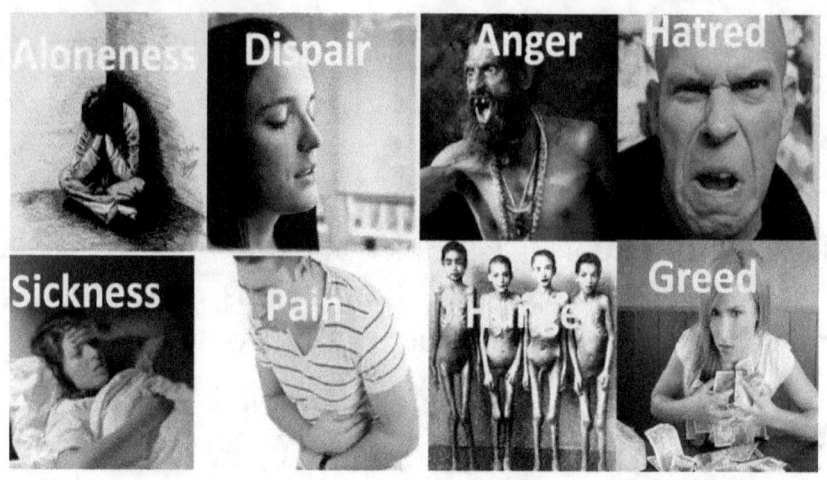

I know you would not think that feeling sorry for yourself would be a horrible thing, but what was being said has relevance to us today and it is truly horrible. None of these things can increase hope, love, charity, empathy, love, or faith. None of these things can help you gain happiness. Remember how the Taoists described it again.

They indicated that to live a life that is meaningful one must think of himself as an empty vessel. [Forget about self to experience and gain TRUE life].

Zoroastrian Method for Happiness

Too much sinfulness	Pouring water in the dark
Sneezing after a prayer	Not killing a frog
Not obeying a priest	Walking barefoot
Unnatural intercourse	Female disobedience
Not getting an adopted son	Allowing sunshine on fire

Ancient Egyptians May Help

58

I didn't see how those things would guide you to happiness, but maybe the ancient Egyptian text will help. Here is what they were supposed to stay away from.

Cursing God	Committing sodomy
Killing animals	Piercing your skin
Violent Stealing	Forgetting Mau-Taui

OK! Maybe I will stay more with Jewish and Christian details. They seem to be more useful as we try to expand our soul to gain happiness. I suppose some would say abstaining from any of these would make you gain more true happiness. But some of these last ones are just silly.

Soul Expansion

With that let's look at the soul or what many call "sub-consciousness". It may be better defined as understanding of the "unity of the souls controlling our universe" over consciousness of "self". With the new anthropic view of our universe, knowing how critical the dimensions of life are to reality, we must reassert the foundations concerning what this universe is actually defined by.

- *There is a reason a small woman can lift a car off her husband and her bones don't break.*

- *There is a reason Moses and the Egyptian magicians could turn a stick into a snake.*

- *There is a reason reincarnation is not only possible but a requirement of existence.*

- *There is a reason Elijah, Peter, Elisha, and others could walk on top of water without falling in.*

- *There is a reason Jesus told his followers "With the faith of a grain of mustard seed one can change the place where a mountain stands." [He was not saying mustard-seeds had all this power, he was saying if we let ourselves allow our souls to take control, we can EVEN change what we typically consider reality.]*

- *There is a reason why an idiot savant can play a piano without lessons.*

- ***There is a reason*** *why some empathetic gesture like giving up your set to a woman seems to make everyone feel better.*

Let's look at this very critical quality of life. As I keep saying this is a little confusing part of Life that has NO understanding or desire for self-preservation, sexual urges, procreation, survival, and gratification which is somewhere between the subconscious and the debase conscious thoughts to gain comfort, greed, selfishness, and all the other carnal desires that tie us to this "reality". The functions are machine-like because they are simply the person or mind's reaction to stimuli totally set in this reality.

The soul portion of life is freedom FROM our carnal nature and the pathway to happiness.

The more powerful this portion of life is the more interaction one can have in controlling his destiny and the destiny of those around him and the more intense can be his happiness.

One thing of note with all dimensional elements that make up existence in this universe, the higher the vibrational frequency, the more control that component has on the environment. Low frequency "matter" makes small atoms [like helium] which don't affect much at all, but massive atoms [like Uranium] represent very high frequencies and they affect our environment greatly. Low frequency photonic vibrations [like radio waves] have little effect, but high frequency vibrations [like cosmic rays] blast through our universe to affect many things. With "soul" vibrations high frequencies can change our reality and low frequencies only view our reality.

Does our "soul" add to or take away from our universe?
If we did not think about something would it disappear?

These questions have haunted philosophers for ages along with the following even more curious question. While the first question has been generally proven over hundreds of experiments and the whole Relativity Theory, a second one is not so easy to test.

When you die does your subconscious die?

If you die, your subconscious energy cannot halt. Your soul continues to insure our reality continues according to Anthropics and Quantum Physics [Oh yes; and the Bible]. The items around us allow our souls to synchronize with the universe so to speak. When our body dies, our soul naturally has more "freedom".

We become part of the universe and add to it with a vibrational union in some way----or our soul sleeps. It is not known by this author which souls sleep and which ones remain active, but that is for another day.

What About Bugs?

Life does not necessarily mean consciously aware life. It is only life. Grass, for instance, is alive, but, most likely not conscious, an amoeba lives, but acts mechanically and it seems to have no consciousness and certainly no sub-consciousness. On and on we could go separating living and consciously aware. The reason we can separate them is that they are very different. Like the relationship of electricity and magnetism, self and soul are very much related. **Aether**, for instance, is not "matter", it is the potential for matter. **"Electricity"** is not "photonic energy", it is the potential for photonic or electromagnetic energy. **What we could call Life** is not cognizant life; it is the potential for conscious awareness. Let me give you an example that everyone can relate to.

Bugs cannot attain true Happiness

Vibration And The Brain

I know you are struggling with the concept that if you become less conscious, the universe is somehow affected, but the idea that our consciousness is interconnected with the universe is not a new one. Even the concept that vibration controls the level of consciousness is not new. While the concept isn't new, new studies in vibrations and the affects to or by the brain are popping up just about every day. Let's look at the list of changes in the brain caused or described vibrationally. I'm talking about the alpha, beta, delta, theta and gamma brainwaves and how they affect us. To test and determine what vibrations affected the brain in what ways, there have been 2 major methods deployed currently. Both of these are audio entrapment methods. That is they allow the brain to interpret much lower frequencies than those actually transmitted.

By moving the thoughts of the brain away from "reality" all sorts of things begin to happen. Pain is removed, stress is relieved, and memory gets better.

Modifying brainwave patterns is a way to enhance happiness.

Two Testing Methods

The first method is called modulation. This method simply modulates any music or tone very slightly. The brain senses the modulation and interprets that as its control function. When these modulations are subsonic, the brain appears to be modified. People begin to think more clearly, pain is reduces, sometimes a feeling of uncertainty evolves.

The second method, binaural interpretation, is similar to the first but is accomplished by sending slightly different frequencies in each ear. The brain picks up on this difference and uses the difference in its normal excitation. Another name for this is INFRATONICS. I tried this method and it is really amazing how well one can remove his "self" portion simply by tuning his brain into a more submissive level. Unfortunately this is not a permanent solution as modifying or restriction information from the brain to allow the wisdom from the soul to generate understanding is difficult. There is a reason many religions push meditation in a number of forms including yoga, prayer, meditational tones and the like. These mask our "SELF" and therefore we can understand and build the control of our Soul. Examples of Infratonic emission equipment is shown below.

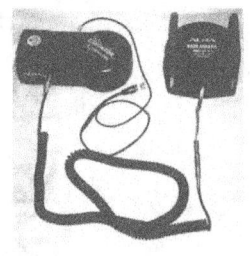

Qui Gong Machine-Certainly there have been blinking lights, mechanical vibration, and magnetic modulation methods, but the audio methods are extremely easy to accomplish. The Infratonic Qui Gong Machine, for instance, was developed out of scientific research in Beijing China which studied natural healers and found that most powerful healers were able to emit a strong infrasonic (low frequency sound) signal from their hands. The sound emitted from average individuals was only a hundredth as strong. The "Infratonic", is now used by 1% of all doctors in the United States and it is believed that it also is an audio modulating device. The Qui Gong Devices are shown below.

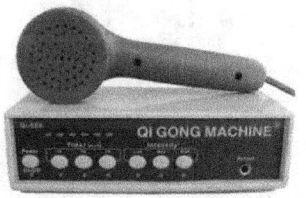
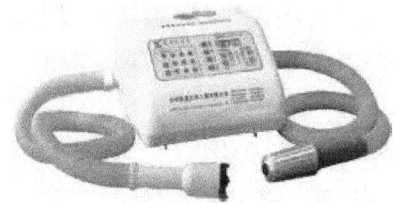

Krell Helmet-A Dr. Keely designed something called the Krell Helmet that relied on electromagnetic fields generated in the helmet. I don't know how successful this machine was, but it illustrates the point that everyone is trying to artificially excite different levels of consciousness and some are beginning to get success. The concept was to generate electromagnetics in a subsonic vibrational level by modulation to cause the brain to react differently. Some indicated this method also had similar results to others identified here. A Krell treatment is shown below.

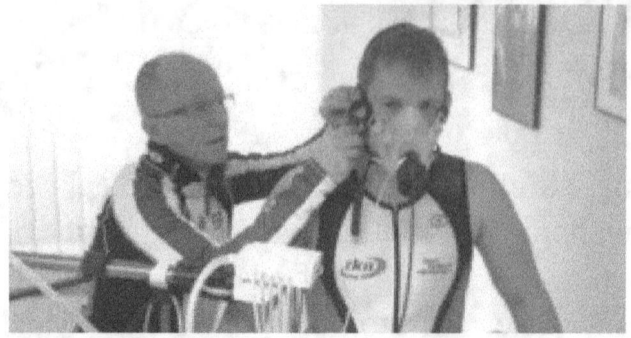

Trans-Cranial Magnetic Stimulation-Before we go on let me bring up one more example that is being used around the world today. By simply taking a magnet and moving it across our brain in a figure eight pattern at a slow rate, we now can reduce stress, pain, increase healing and learning. Called Trans-cranial magnetic stimulation, it was first found that rats learned faster from this process. Today, thousands change the way their "SELF" vibrates by using this vibrating magnetic input instead of the harder to control subsonic emission. Images below show some of the techniques and equipment used in this type of brain modification. This seems to be more like degaussing your brain like we used to have to do with large tube televisions.

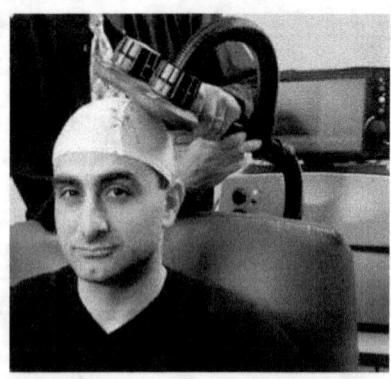
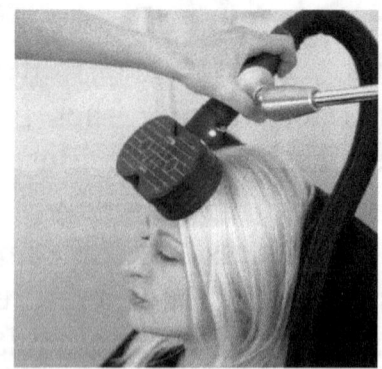

Sphincter Resonator-Not everyone has gained success as can be illustrated with something called Sphincter Resonance. In the 1960s, somebody discovered the resonating frequency of the sphincter. Presumably, this team created a device later called an "Anal Sphincter Resonator". It was, supposedly, kind of like a musical organ. The idea was to intensify the "suspense" in movies whenever "Danger" was about to be portrayed. BACKFIRE and more BACKFIRE. Apparently it caused the entire audience to soil themselves. The specific group of tones generated by this contraption has been referred to as a 'Brown Note' for some reason that I am not going into at this time. The specific notes have been lost over time, so I'm sure one of these mishaps will occur again in the future, which brings us to this table. [No image]

Type	Freq. (Hz)	Normal Reactions
Epsilon	<0.5	Extraordinary states of consciousness, High states of meditation, Ecstatic states of consciousness, High-level inspiration states, Spiritual insight, Out-of-body experiences, Suspended animation.
Delta	0.2 to 4 Hz	Confusion, boosting intuition, Deep sleep, Lucid dreaming, Increased immune functions, Hypnosis, Anti-aging, Increased intuition, Inner being & personal growth, Trauma recovery, Near death experience, Blissful "being" state
Theta	4 – 7 Hz	Arousal, Deep relaxation, Increased memory, Creativity, Hypnagogic state, Access to subconscious images, Reduced blood pressure, Profound inner peace, emotional healing, Inner wisdom, Faith, psychic abilities, Twilight sleep learning, Vivid mental imagery, Military remote viewing
Alpha	8 – 12 Hz	Relaxation, Meditation, Light relaxation, Positive thinking, Creative problem solving, Mood elevation, Stress reduction, Intuitive insights, Daydreams, Calm, relaxed, Lucid mental states, Tranquility, Detachment
Beta	12 – 30 Hz	Alertness, Anxious thinking, Active concentration Analytical problem solving, Judgment, Decision making, Increased mental ability, Focus, Good for absorbing information passively, Treating Hyperactivity, Sensorimotor Rhythm, Outer awareness, Arousal, Dendrite growth,
Gamma	30 – 100 +	Motor functions heightened, Boosted memory, Enhanced perception of reality, Binding of all senses, Increased compassion, High-level information processing, Natural antidepressant, Positive thoughts, Higher energy levels, Decision making in a fear situation, Muscle tension, Release of growth hormone, muscles, Recovery from injuries, Rejuvenation effects

The previous table shows some of the findings of researchers trying to modify the conscious mind externally. While there are specific frequencies that cause each of these effects, I'm not going to go into that detail in this book. My main objective right now is to show that vibrational fields greatly affect consciousness. Don't worry that these frequencies are so very low in frequency compared to the super high frequencies needed to convert matter into different substances. We don't know why these low frequencies "activate" various parts of our brain and consciousness. These are simply observations. While the military is experimenting with broadcasting subsonic waves to affect brainwaves and enhance the Delta levels [to confuse and put fear in an enemy], many are now trying to tap into meditative states and learning ability by transmitting the 40 Hertz level. What we are finding is that simple stereo speakers may be the best tool to introduce these GAMMA enhancers. A 200-hertz tone is shot into one ear and a 240-hertz sound is transmitted into the other ear. The brain gets both of these frequencies and tries to mix them together to understand the sound. When the 2 frequencies a beat together, the output becomes the difference or 40-Hertz and the brain begins to learn faster.

Catalyst Frequencies

It is believed these are merely catalyst frequencies and repeatability of experiments depends of the person directing the experiments. His consciousness affects the results. This is why people have not been able to reconstruct the Sphincter Resonator-----LUCKILY. Can you imagine what this would be like in the wrong hands?

Brain Vibrations

The reason I brought up ability to change the way our "self" brain thinks is that it describes how sensitive our consciousness is to vibration. The reason is simple. Consciousness is a vibrational dimension and brainwave studies are not the only way to recognize the vibrational characteristics. A second way is something called "chakra" by Buddhists so let's look at some of these mystical things. According to the believers and the testing skeptics there are at least seven of these chakras or levels of consciousness. As someone increases his chakra, we are told he feels a vibration all around and inside. The vibration intensifies as higher levels are reached. They are sort of represented by the diagram below with the first being the lowest level of being.

- Root, Chakra--- "consciousness of Survival"
- Sacral Chakra --- "Consciousness of Sex"
- Solar Plexus Chakra --- "Consciousness of Self"
- Heart Chakra --- "Consciousness of love"
- Throat, Chakra --- "Consciousness of the truth"
- Third Eye Chakra --"Consciousness of inner being"
- Crown, Chakra ---"Consciousness of the spirit world"

I know it sounds like I'm some guru from India talking about chakras, but it is a convenient way to discuss this dimensional component so I'm going to continue. I'm not putting on the towel on my head, but I may hum a little as I write this section.

Remember what this is all about is the rejection of the Self, Survival, Sex debased thoughts that restrict, wisdom, and enhanced control over our environment to essential do what the Bible recommend.

If you want to live you must die [so to speak].

Sorry for bringing this up several times, but let's say a girl witnesses her father being pinned under a car. She immediately rejects self, sex, and survival and this allows her to "move mountains"--- or a car in this situation. As soon as she realizes what she did, reality goes back to normal. For an instant all the fear and hurt are gone and she is in another place.

An idiot savant who is not as in touch with this reality taps into the "universal knowledge of music. His brain and muscle memory all are modified and he immediately "knows" how to play a violin or a piano. Luckily, his rejection of reality continues as his body catches up to the new found knowledge. Happiness fills in where rejection of the world is changed to music.

Elisha or Peter walk on water by doing the same thing their bodies no longer were heavy enough to sink. As they walked, they were filled with comfort and happiness.

John Hutchison's experiment making a bowling ball rise off the table is the same, but he simple introduce ultra-high beat frequencies on the scene with his equipment to momentarily change reality in the "focused" area. I must say that John typically has trouble duplicating his results, but they are still something special. Like another researcher who had similar results, John Keely, they did not understand how very important the vibrational level of the observer was on their results. They also did not recognize the feeling of happiness that filled them as the experiments defied logic.

Sphincter Resonance- Even forcing the loss of bowel control shows a remarkable control over the environment due to enhancement of our soul vibration resonance. [OK; forget that one and let's talk about death.]

Except for the last one, changing vibrational patterns can allow for more happiness.

Life/Death

Let me talk briefly about the three dimensions of life that turns a lump of DNA that has been energized by the electromagnetic forces of our perceived reality into life. I am purposely repeating particular elements of this to allow you time and repetition to increase understanding. I am sorry for those already having a keen awareness, but some need to become accustomed to what is possible very different than what they thought life was. I will spend more time with both life and death later to help that part sink in after we study time to get an understanding of how life really works. As I explained life requires the combination of self, soul, and spirit as described in the Bible. Don't go thinking that because this book has excerpts from the Bible that it is not a science book. There are other examples that we could use, but many already know the Biblical history.

*1 Thessalonians 5:23- "And the very God of peace sanctify you wholly; and I pray God your whole **spirit and soul and body** be preserved blameless unto the coming of our Lord Jesus Christ."*

Yes your "self" dies, but the soul and spirit live on to gain additional "selfs" during the course of time, so don't think this is trying to confuse you.

Releasing the Soul For Happiness

Like all dimensional elements of our universe life has a "potential" for its essence when there was no vibration and when it vibrated too fast, it sort of goes "beyond our reality" as pure gravity or pure magnetism or the **released soul** of a living person. The spirit is that part of life that goes beyond our universe so let's ignore this for a while. I will address it later. The "Self" is the potential for cognizant life and the "soul" is what can go beyond our reality as we venture away for this thing we can call "self".

Soul Governor

Remember that little girl that picked up the car off her dad? This is sort of saying the same thing. Our soul is, *generally*, tied to our perceived reality, but it also is outside this reality. If you remember The Matrix movies, it might be something like that where our soul can see the truth behind the façade we recognize all around us. This reality is kind of like a governor on a motor that keeps it from going too fast and destroying itself. It builds a reality around something that has been called the "resonance of life". If you are uncomfortable with resonance it essentially means, everything in the universe is comfortable at a certain main vibrational level. Remember, if matter vibrates too fast, it ceases to be matter and the same is true of photonic energy that becomes magnetism. Well--Life is the same. If we [or our self-soul wave] vibrate too quickly, we will cease to be. That is, we will cease to be in this universe. The faster we vibrate, the more we control our surrounding "reality" just like mass gets more powerful as it vibrates faster and electromagnetic waves become more violent forces like gamma waves, etc. Everything in our universe is tightly affixed to everything else, but that does not mean everything is RIGIDLY defined. What is does mean is that the faster we vibrate the happier we CAN become.

Vibrate Faster than Others

If we can somehow vibrate faster than the "life reality around us, we have more control over the reality, but at the same time less interest in this reality so it is a two edged sword. On a small scale, you would recognize that if someone is "meditating" he loses his awareness of the things around him. That's what Jesus was stating in the book of Matthew. The person who, for an instant, gains tremendous power to help someone out from under a car is done much the same way.

Walked on Water and Move Mountains

Don't believe Peter, and Elisha, and Elijah, and Jesus didn't walk on water because someone said it's impossible. Don't think that you can't leave your body simply because it seems odd. Don't think that when Jesus told his people that _**faith**_ _as small as a grain of mustard-seed is all that is required to move mountain_s was a lie because you had no understanding of what the word "faith" was as you kept getting it confused with religion.

Faith has NOTHING to do with religion

Certainly there were descriptions of "Faith-in God", "Faith in Jesus", etc. but this verse was talking about "normal faith" or it would have been said differently. Let me just tell you the Biblical description of what Jesus told his followers. This comes from "Hebrews".

***Hebrews 11:1**- "Faith is the <u>assurance of things hoped for</u>, the <u>evidence of things not seen</u>"*

Jesus told his followers that even "**NORMAL Faith**" could change the construct of reality. That was not **faith in Jesus**, he was telling them about Anthropic Science before anyone had even heard of it. He was God incarnate, but he told us ***"We"*** *can move mountains just by telling them to move if he says we can.* In the Anthropic expansion of physics, it is not only possible, it can be considered a requirement that is stifled by people simply "enjoying" carnal life with its sex, satisfaction, pride, power, and all the things that we begin to lose as we gain power to control our environment and start feeling true happiness. One must abandon, self, sex, and survival to allow ANY modification of the vibrational level of life, so to speak, gain more happiness, and allow a better control over one's reality. The following images of someone walking on water, turning water into wine, and Moses' staff turning into a snake, or not going against reality, they are just going against "normal" reality. We want to go beyond all that.

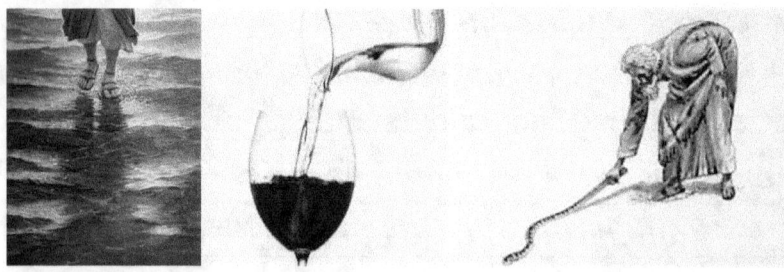

As we gain new levels of happiness, it can continue even after what we call death. Before we get there, we will need look at the three elements of ourselves in another light.

Egyptians and Freud

As I mentioned, the "Christian 3 person in one" is universal in the ancient world and pretty much in today's world, so I hope none of this is too strange. The Egyptians had the <u>Ba, Ka, and shadow</u> while Sigmund Freud had his <u>Ego, ID, and Superego</u>.

Self-Of these three we understand the Self or the Ka or the ID the best. We see it every day. This is the part of life we can call carnal. Emphasis of these carnal elements is what can doom a soul and reduce our ability to achieve true happiness. While it is the main component of what we see as life it is the key to misery. I'm not talking about a lake of fire, here, I simply talking about the wonders that can be achieved with the "faith of a grain of mustard-seed".

Soul- Called the EGO or the BA, the soul is the MAIN part of an individual. Don't ignore the soul. Don't ignore the most important part of your existence. It is the part that won't die. Freud's view is provided below left.

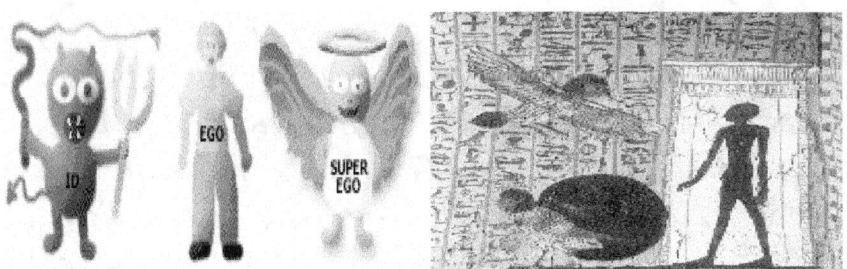

Egyptian Life Dimensions

The Egyptians essentially said the same thing as the Jews except they called the dimensions of the person the Ka [body], *baa, sahu* and *akh* [the soul or independent attribute] , and the Shut [Shadow] the part belonging to the nether world [That would be the closest to the "spirit"]. The previous image right shows how they would draw these components. The Sahu is the flying part completely free of the body. The Ka is shown in the jar, while in this reality, it is completely shut out from the "Real" existence that the soul can experience. The shadow was, sort of, in between; neither here nor there. For the Egyptians, true happiness could only be obtained by the Baa or Sahu. This is still true today.

Egyptian Book of the Dead on the Ka/Body/Self-_The Osiris X, may he rest in peace, knows **the names of your ka**, the **aspect of your soul** that abides in the ground: Nourishing ka, ka of food, lordly ka, ka the ever-present helper, ka which is a pair of kas begetting more kas, healthy ka, sparkling ka, victorious ka ,ka the strong, ka that strengthens the sun each day to rise from the world of the dead, ka of shining resurrection, powerful ka, effective ka._

The Sahu or Soul Egyptian Book of the Dead on the Sahu/Soul-_"I go round about heaven and sail in the presence of Ra, I look upon all the beings who have knowledge. Hail, Ra, I who goes round about in the sky, I say, O Osiris in truth, that I am the **Sahu of the god,** and I beseech you not to let me be driven away, nor to be cast upon the wall of blazing fire. The Osiris knows the names of your Sahu, the form in which you travel our world - the sun. Sahu pure of body, health-embodying ba, ba bright and unharmed, ba of magic, ba who causes himself to appear, male ba, ba whose warm energy encourages copulating."_ [This description is exactly what I have been talking about. The soul lives beyond our body or self.] That brings us to the "Shadow".

The Papyrus of Nu *-O mighty One, when he is adored, great one among* bas, *greatly respected* ba *inspiring the gods with awe when he has appeared on his great throne: then may he prepare the path, justified, his ba,* ***and his shadow****, may they be well provided for. Let not be shut in my soul, let not be fettered my "shadow", let the way be opened for* ***my soul and for my "shadow"****, may it see the great god,* [Unlike the body, the shadow was not bound to the grave and could go where the body could not. In New Kingdom, tombs it was at times depicted leaving the body accompanied by the *ba*-bird. Clearly the shadow was not the soul. These concepts were slightly different that those of the nomadic Jewish people, but I think you can see the similarity. In modern times, people have struggled with the definitions because it seemed to give them less control over their environment rather than more. Sigmund Freud, for instance, tried to redefine the elements of life into his own concept to try to make it seem that this reality could hold the essence of the three dimensions of life.

Freud Life Dimensions

Sigmund Freud tried to connect the differences in characterizing a person without using ancient religion to guide him. He came close, but almost missed important aspects. In Freud's model of the psyche there were the ID (instinctive unconscious), the Ego (organized, conscious), and the Superego (moralizing, not entirely unconscious) form an interactive framework which work together in the mind. Here is what he had to say. *"One of the fundamental functions of the Ego is Reality Testing – reaching into the real world to see if what is believed to be the case actually proves out – but this does not bear full fruit until the Ego has become Autonomous... substantially set free from inner conflicts between the ID and Superego."*

The ID was the evil characterization just as the Ka and the self are completely carnal and separated from understanding outside the body. The Superego was close to the definition we must place on the Spirit portion of the body; sort of the HOLY component of a person. Of course the ID or self is not specifically evil, whatever evil is. It is simply carnal. With that as a background, let's get into a new description of our universe so you will see how everything has a place and everything is required for our universe to operate.

Conservation of Life Force

Have you ever heard of conservation of energy? As it turns our very little can be ended. This includes life-force. From the concept of conservation of life-force we interpret the continuation of the Soul and spirit after what we call death. Life force is conserved just like Energy and Time.

Conservation of Energy-I think I had better go over this again. According to Einstein, *vibrational nothingness associated with mass and light continued outward from a central point and escaped the limits of the universe at infinity. This means that sooner or later, all will be dark and no mass or energy will exist.* While that would certainly be in the distant future, it still makes me uncomfortable and it really doesn't make sense that existence is not renewing. Additionally, conservation of energy laws would be violated. <u>As the light energy hits the end of our universe and leaves, it is immediately replenished.</u> Everything else in the universe renews and we can, pretty much, be assured that the same is true of mass and light [electro-magnetic stress]. Everything in this universe is continually renewed.

If energy is renewed, <u>life must be renewed</u> in a similar way so we can gain information about ourselves by comparison to non-living energies.

Conservation of Time-Time must also be rejuvenative. Here's the deal.

Time must go backward while it is going forward.

I know that sounds weird. This is especially interesting after death as one is locked in the relativistic arena called the "speed of light". It is so weird, having the backward time-dual makes you wonder strange things. Does death come first and a person gets younger or is it the other way around? Are there just snapshots in time and only the now is real? If the now isn't real, are our "selfs" real? It is that type of thinking that is going either mess you up or help you understand what the thing we call reality IS. Maybe Chromosomes can help us understand happiness in this fleeting moment.

Dead Chromosomes

A dead chromosome and a live one look the same and have the same characteristics. The sugars are the same, the links and bonds are the same.

Something outside the chromosome makes it alive.

This thing outside the DNA and Chromosomes is what we can call life. DNA causes sensation, anger, hunger and sexual urges, but life is more than that. In particular, it is the "self" driven by the "soul" that actually can bring us intense happiness. As one set of chromosomes or a person becomes dead, another seems to become alive. I know you are thinking there are more people alive today than during the old days, so this **"Conservation of Life"** doesn't look like it will hold water. This is because you are not identifying life without self. Just because a soul has "no body" does not mean there is no life in it. In fact, the most intense happiness may come as the soul is released from the body for a time. It simply cannot experience what we call reality just like gravity can never become matter. We can think of this state as "going the speed of light".

We know that "at the speed of Light" all life is suspended; you do not age at all as this reality is completely gone so all that going backwards in time doesn't mean anything to our souls.

When one talks about people vibrating, it is both simple and almost impossible to understand. Everything---I mean everything, is made of vibration. This includes all matter, all electro-magnetics, all nuclear energy, all photons, even all life forces and those we would consider dead. That by itself is not enough information. The second thing is that live and "dead people" control what we believe to be reality. As such they experience happiness as the entire reality is affected by their vibrational resonance. I know all this "soul with no body" stuff is bizarre, but I want you to understand when we say man was made in God's Truine image, each of his 3 entities are bot together AND separate.

Reality Check

Let me make a simple observation. ---The color RED-- what is it? The answer, of course is vibration and more specifically, electromagnetic vibration just wiggling all over the place. While it is wiggling at a certain rate, other colors and things that are completely invisible are vibrating at different frequencies in a constant time observation. Why in the world do we see RED when it is only vibrating nothingness??? The answer has to do with that Anthropic Universe things I mentioned before. Here is a definition of this important science.

Participatory Anthropic is the science that studies how our linked consciousnesses define observations to vibrations. [Notice I did not say "seems to". In fact, our group consciousnesses invent ALL of the [carnal] reality. Carnal meaning the reality we see, smell, hear, feel, etc. As we vibrate above this "set" level, we will enhance our happiness.

It is this collection of "Souls" that determine that any time 635nm waves are sensed by rods and cones in the eye that we would ALL establish the color RED as part of the immediate reality.---Eliminate all the souls and RED is gone.

Reality Without Coordinated Resonance Of SOULS

The "invention of the souls" is what we call reality!!! Imagine a reality where all you feel is vibration, there is no light as it is just vibrations and there is no distance to allow you to know where you are. If you try to interact with another SELF, their perceptions of vibrations are totally different and you don't even know the 2 of you are "nearby". What good is the vibrational cluster of mass or the vibrations of time all around without the "stage" we call reality? The question remains; is reality real?

Reality Isn't Real

If you have ever heard the terms "Power of Positive Thinking", "Think and Grow Rich", and all other concepts of the 70s which I brought up before; they tried to convince you that how you consciously view reality will affect reality. The concepts are not only true, they make you happy. In the Anthropic World if you have faith of a grain of mustard-seed, you can move a mountain, as Jesus said thousands of years ago and you can walk on water as demonstrated by Elijah, Elisha, Peter, and Jesus so many years ago. With the Anthropic Principle, science and religion can act as a single tool for us to understand God, the universe, and ourselves. The dead souls and live people "souls" shape and mold reality. Let me give you an example.

Eating

Today we know that what something looks like changes greatly what something tastes like. If you see mashed stuff and it tastes crispy, the "mind" quickly determines what it SHOULD BE and viola' it ACTUALLY becomes "that" to the taste buds, touch sensors, and emotion centers determining that you like of don't like what you are eating and level of satisfaction you feel after feeling the substance. The taste bud only looks for a chemical so it can vibrate differently. One taste bud wiggles from salt, another from a sour, etc. nothing really determines taste beyond these minor elements. The wiggling is in the form of chemical combinations allowed by structure. If one of the "particles" can attach to the crystal, it gets bigger and vibrates fasters making an electrical differential which is "felt" back at the nerve centers in the brain and it is magically determined if it was a good or bad taste. This imaginary "taste" makes you happy.

Have you wondered how in the world some people "love" the taste of nasty stuff and you can't stand it? If there was a reality to taste, all would either like the brain response or not. Taste is simply not real.

The same can be said for seeing colors, sensing Aether, looking at beauty, etc. It is all pretty much fake and only "defined" by how we interacted with this "reality" over the years.

Perception of Being

What is the perception of being? One answer is seeing the things around us and interacting with them. A problem is that there are no real things around us but simply vibrating nothingnesses as Einstein and others have proven. The forces established by the vibrations give us the "perception" of mass. The same thing happens with everything in the universe.

"Perceived" Electricity and Sight

For this discussion, let's look at sight. Vibrating of something we defined as electro-magnetivity makes a chemical change in our rods and cones of the eye. The chemical changes produce something we call electricity which excites portions of the brain. Everyone uses this electricity stuff to define everything, but it doesn't exist. It is a "potential to do something" by definition. It does not exist except for something we call work that requires some outside intervention with this "invisible potential". It is only the magnetic field produced as the electricity changes that makes it real to us. While it is changing or "VIBRATING" it is in our perceived world. The brain remembers what it perceives from the changing electrical signal and simply "defines" what we call sight. Just think what our world would be like if we could REALLY see what enters our eyes. The things we think we see are just reflections of some external light source rather than the actual object. When the external light source is removed, the objects we see are removed from view. Try to remember that the "real" reality comes from a thing you can't see called the SOUL. The entire universe is controlled by the joining of souls all defining away.

Our existence or what we perceive as our existence is a combined implication of all in existence. This includes existence when we are DEAD.

Let me give you one important example called Mauve. The color we call Mauve does not exist. If we look at the color spectrum starting with ultraviolet to violet, blue, green, yellow, red and infrared. Before ultraviolet is radio waves and beyond infrared there are X-rays but red never mixes with violet-----IT CAN'T. There is no vibration associated with Mauve, but somehow we see this impossibility because what we see is not what we actually see.

I suppose we could say Mauve makes us happy.

It's kind of like faith.

Faith and Reality

I know I have laid out this anthropic world and told you generally about how the universe is modified by people and you have totally believed what I have been saying because it makes so much sense. You are skeptical, but hopefully I have described this reality in enough ways to allow you to try to expand from it or with it to assume self-actualization and finally happiness. At best, you looked up a sight on Anthropic Universe and found out that one way of looking at it is to sense that <u>the universe was simply made for us</u>. God grabbed the universe and modified it so that people could be created. All the creationists roared, but that is simply not the end and if you try to define people that way you simply have something like mashed potatoes oozing around to fill limitations of the universe.

What anthropic physics really shows is that people can modify the universe [to an extent]. In the process, they can gain happiness.

Over time, the universe, quite naturally is shifted to be in line with the needs of people. If you remember the center of the universe is on Earth somewhere and that is impossible because the "Big Bang explosion happened at the center of the universe. By the physical findings, we KNOW that the beginning was not made until well after we came along. What I mean by that is everything in the universe is defined for the PRESENT reality and the ends can change [beginning and end] to confirm our PRESENT reality. I'm going to tell you how this also affects what you call death, but you first need to broaden you awareness so the details will be more useful to you.

Faith is not Faith

Remember, Jesus told his disciples that with faith of a grain of mustard seed one could move mountains. As I stated before he was not talking about faith in him or he would have said it. If he wasn't talking about faith in him, what was he talking about? That, my friends, hopefully, is becoming more evident as we go along. Buddhist monks, for instant, have substantial amounts of faith, but they have no regard for Jesus, God incarnate. These monks have done miraculous things. The Gurus seem to have something we could identify as faith, but they also have no specific faith in Jesus. Many of the faith healers around the world don't profess any specific religious order. The Egyptian magicians Jannes and Jambres had no faith in God, but they could turn a stick into a snake. On and on we could go. Faith, as discussed by Jesus in his plea to his followers was something besides faith in Jesus. I am certainly not saying don't have faith in the living God and God Incarnate. That is a different subject. This is simply saying Faith allows us to change what we might call Space Resonance.

Resonance

I have been talking about resonance throughout this book, but let's take one more look as resonance of all dimensions together is what we call reality. Let me back up a little and restate resonance for this application in the words of Dr. Milo Wolff who is one of the leading master physicists who has greatly extended Einstein's initial work into a "usable" platform. My comments are in "bold".

"Resonance is composed of a spherical IN-wave which converges to the center **[of the universe and comes from a different universe as a component of the operational dimension dynamo]** *and an OUT-wave which diverges from the center* **[of the universe and makes up what I call the structural dimensional dynamo]**. *Their separate amplitudes are* **[*close to*]** *infinite at the centers.* **[Like all other resonance factors in the universe, how close they are to being infinite can be considered the "quality of resonance".]** *When combined, the two waves form a standing-wave which has a finite amplitude at the center. The standing wave* **[*appears*]** *to be the structure of the electron. The inward and outward waves* **[*sort-of*]** *provide communication with other matter of the universe. Spin of the electron is a result of the reversal of the IN wave at the center to become the OUT wave."*

While there are still limitations, this, this definition helps us interpret how an adjacent universe "establishes" resonance in this world. The more we communicate with an adjacent universe the faster our vibrational resonance becomes and its quality rises.

Quality of Resonance

Let me explain this "quality of resonance" a little because it is this quality that will allow one to expand how a soul interacts with reality. In electro-magnetics, quality of resonance describes the difference between the effect of a circuit outside its resonance frequency and that which can be described when it is in resonance. If a crystal is excited with a vibration that is half of the frequency it likes, it may vibrate a little and nothing more, but if it is hit with the vibration it likes, it begins to self-oscillate substantially. Just think of a tuning fork and how it always sounds the same when struck. That is its resonance and the longer it makes the sound describes its "quality" of resonance. In the electro-magnetic world, this "quality of resonance" depends on many things including what the crystal is attached to, how well the crystal is cut and how homogeneous the crystal is. In the electron or particle world, the same things can be surmised. Purity of the particle and the things that surround the particle affect how close to infinity the standing wave appears.

Resonance and Matter

I guess you are wondering why I even brought up this resonance in the first place, but ---

Resonance holds matter together, it holds time together, and it holds life together.

If enough electrons are in an area that are sensing similar in-waves, they align together just like a crystal. One could say that atoms are resonant plugs that are held together by "like vibrations". Scientists found these things called gluons which seem to act in opposition to other particles and quasi-particles. Gluons hold quarks together. Three quarks and an unknown number of gluons are called an electron. **Gluons are quasi-particles [fermions] that have a negative gravity.** That is, the farther the quarks move away from the gluons the STRONGER the gluon attraction becomes. It is sort of, like the quarks are inside and invisible piece of matter that has gravity. The closer they get to the surface of this invisible piece of matter, the more the gravity affects the quarks. The center of what we call a gluon would be the resonance point of what an electron whose resonance is defined by the vibrational characteristics of its component parts. I know that was a mouthful so let me state it differently.

Gluons are not odd, they are simply invisible. One can say that they are an in-wave and out-wave collision; sort of the core of an atom.

Life Resonance

There is a reason I keep bringing up religious testimony. I want you to see that true science and religion both ARE the same and I'm going to let you in on a secret. Consciousness/ life/ and death all act the same.

If we wish to affect the universe more and have a higher quality of resonance, we must become pure and surround ourselves with things that allow this pureness.

OK! I can't exactly define what pureness is, but prayer and meditation is probably more important to our quality of resonance and our capability of affecting the universe than one would initially believe.

Who Cares About Resonance?

Why have I even brought up resonance? If a vibration node gets larger or smaller it shouldn't matter to us. Right? ---Wrong!

By changing resonance of reality, you gain true happiness.

With that let's see how we can change resonance.

Soul Enhancement Levels

As I mentioned briefly some call the vibrational changes in like "Chakras". Each change or increase in vibrational resonance---INCREASES our feeling of happiness. We first start with levels that are many times below the natural resonance of reality.

Survival and Sex

Whether we admit it or not, every one of us battles these things every day. The most basic root chakra is triggered when you get hungry and the sex one, well; it shows up from time to time; many times in the most awkward times. I'm sure you recognize that these components of our life are, pretty much, uncontrollable and they should never be associated with conscious control. It is true many use sex as an entertainment that attempts all types of positioning, unusually methodologies, and even unusual partners in an attempt at gaining some type of "satisfaction" a person believes they are missing. The same happens to the binge eater who eats well after any primal requirement for survival has completely gone. Except for the pure gluttony of it all, these "feelings" run <u>parallel to conscious thought always ready to break or modify our consciousness</u>. I only brought them up again because some identify them as consciousness levels. A rule of thumb might be if it is associated directly with pleasure, pain, desire, or self-preservation, it is part of this dimension of your life. Some self-preservation elements such as moving your hand away from a burning flame is identified as autonomous. I would contend that other things are autonomous as well.

Self, Love, and Truth

If you can get past those or begin to ignore those urges you start considering self-worth and even love. Most people spend most of the time going back and forth between the lower 2 and the others. It's sort of like a yo-yo or they interact simultaneously. Slow vibrations, higher vibrations, slower vibrations, higher vibrations and still higher vibrations when someone pays me a compliment or a figure out why a light bulb turns on in the refrigerator or I answer one of those "Are You Smarter Than a 5th Grader" questions. Answering one of the "Jeopardy" questions correctly might even get you into the heart chakra.

Real Love

The heart chakra is a vibrational level associated with "Real" love rather than the sexual one. I believe that an ameba and a tree have no capability of love, but they are still alive. Sometimes this "heart" level happens naturally for a brief time and you can't seem to even think about yourself at all. If you work at it you can get to this level periodically throughout a day and look at people with true look. The Bible called it *loving people as you love yourself.* Anyway, most just think they get into love and it is more basic. That primal type of love puts you below the stomach again. Anyway you must conquer love to some level before you can even get to a point that looks for "real truth" rather than "Vain truth" that we usually accept or desire. Vain truth is a truth to you. You want it to be true so it is. Real truth is a truth that is truth no matter how it affects the event or who thinks it. It is usually not a popular truth or even the one you would hope for. It simply is. Let me give you an example. You like your cooking so the vain truth is you are a good cook. This may not be the absolute truth. Another example might be going to heaven. While the Bible specifically states that *"no one is in heaven yet except for God and the angels"* and *"all are sleeping until Jesus comes back"* and the *"All the dead in Christ [All the souls of the dead who believed in Jesus] rise and meet Jesus in the sky to go to heaven at the same time when Jesus retakes the world"*. Some have a vain truth that their loved ones have been in heaven for hundreds of years before the return of Jesus. Before I go on, I think I had better expand on my example or someone is going to find me and hit me.

What Do You Mean Dead Sleep?

Generally speaking the souls of most dead people SLEEP! For this example let's just say everyone sleeps.

Ecclesiastes 9:5-The soul of the living know that they shall die, but the dead know not anything. They are asleep.

OK! What about when the thief on the cross was told by God Incarnate that he would be in paradise that day?

Luke 23:42-43-And he was saying, "Jesus, remember me when You come in Your kingdom!" And He said to him, "Truly I say to you, today you shall be with Me in Paradise."

Certainly, Jesus did not go to heaven right away and I can tell you it was not a lie. I'm not getting into a long dissertation about what a day is when you are dead, but if you are sleeping, day would be when you wake up so we can tell that the thief, was sleeping after he died until Jesus comes back, but Jesus said "TODAY". Now we have to listen to Einstein again. "If you vibrate the speed of light----NO TIME PACES for you. *What Einstein was really saying is time has no relevance.* Time has no meaning when you are dead unless you somehow interact with this reality and I'm not getting into that. To the thief-vibrating so fast time stood still, when he begins to slow down at the end of day, NO TIME will have passed for him.

John 11:11-44-*He said, and after that He said to them, "Our friend Lazarus sleeps, but I go that I may wake him up." -- Then Jesus said to them plainly, "Lazarus is dead. --- Jesus, cried with a loud voice, "Lazarus, come forth!" And he who had died came out bound hand and foot with grave clothes, and his face was wrapped with a cloth. Jesus said to them, "Loose him, and let him go."* Lazarus could not tell people about the afterlife, because he had not lived one. He had been "as if asleep". Jesus told everyone that death was like sleep. I don't mean a dreaming sleep. I mean a nothingness sleep. Why didn't Lazarus know anything about where he had been? To him he had not been gone.

1 Corinthians 15:40-44-- *Behold, I tell you a secret: we shall not all sleep, but we shall ALL BE CHANGED, IN, MOMENT, in the twinkling of an eye, AT THE LAST TRUMP: for the trumpet shall sound, and the dead [souls] shall be raised incorruptible, and we shall be changed.*

Again, no question about everyone "sleeping" when they are dead until Jesus comes back. Everyone who is dead "in Christ" gets yanked out of their graves to become immortal. The idea that everyone stays asleep in their graves until Jesus comes back is reinforced in "John", "Ecclesiastes" and "Daniel.

John 5:28-*The hour is coming, in which all who are in the graves [sleeping] shall hear his voice, and shall come forth"* Generally speaking those who are dead are STILL sleeping until God comes back.

Daniel 12:2-*Them that sleep in the dust of the earth.*

*Matthew 27:52-"The graves were open and many bodies of the saints who had **fallen asleep** were raised."*

This last verse talks about when Jesus revived himself after his cross death. Not only does it help expand the confirmation of something miraculous happening, it also shows that people are still in [on the earth] after death--- "sleeping". Please don't think that they were yanked out of Heaven to re-inhabit their bodies. Peter reinforces the idea some more in Acts by bringing up David, still in his tomb and not in heaven.

Acts 2:29-34-Men and brother, let me speak freely to you, the patriarch David, he is both dead and buried and his tomb is with us to this day.---For David did not ascend into Heaven." Man oh man! "Why be Christian?" some would say, but Paul states it in the best way. *"When Jesus comes back all the dead people rise and BEGIN their eternal COMFORT".*

The Bible states that when we "end life" God takes the "spirit" portion of "you" and the "self" portion of "You" becomes dust again. That leaves the soul that sleeps, sometimes thousands of years.

Ecclesiastes 12: 7- "Then, shall the dust [dead SELF/body] return to the earth as it was, and [only]the spirit shall return unto God who gave it."

This is talking about dying and saying that when someone dies, his physical part turns to dust and his spirit, is completely separated from it. A person is only made up of a "self" and "Spirit" and a "Soul". The "soul" part is the part that doesn't die. Unfortunately, this is not always the case.

*1 Thessalonians 4:15--This we say unto you by the word of the Lord, that we which are alive and remain unto the coming of the Lord <u>shall not prevent them **which are asleep**</u> [not in heaven], <u>because the Lord Himself shall descend from Heaven with a shout with a voice of the archangel and with the trumpet of God, see the last trumpet, happens with the second coming, the dead in Christ shall rise first</u> and we which are alive and remain shall be caught up together with them in the clouds to meet the Lord in the air so shall we ever be with the Lord comfort one another with these words.*

While people can be awakened from death-sleep, generally speaking, <u>dead people sleep until Jesus comes back or until they are to be reincarnated</u>. To someone who has passed away, there is no sense of time as we understand it as indicated in Luke, just like there is no sense of time when we vibrate at the speed of light. While a number of people have clearly been brought back including Samuel, Melchizedek, Moses, Isaiah, Elijah, Jonah, Job, Paul, and others, there is a strong belief that very few dead people are "disturbed". Some believe there is a larger number of people who "return", but do not believe a second chance is a given and don't believe you will be the same person with the same memories, and the same desires, and the same carnal life. ---- Death does not work that way.

Sorry for the Biblical Description

I'm sorry about the Biblical tirade, but I know this is a sore subject for many and I want you to understand just how important your soul portion is. You must focus on the soul part of you to attain true happiness.--- Certainly if you want to attain happiness after death there are a few

100

other things, but let's continue. People almost never are tuned to this type of consciousness so they accept what their believed truth rather than expanding their awareness.

While this level of consciousness is difficult to achieve, once we get to this level, our hearts will be glowing and happiness will fill our souls.

Let's say you get an openness to understand real truth, there are still 2 more levels of consciousness to be considered.

Who Controls Our Universe?

Before we get to the next one, let me say something that is very important. Anthropics tells us that cognizant observers modify our universe. Some might try to put a dog, worm, a blade of grass, monkey, or even a fetus in the mix so here is the rule of cognition. It is not "knowing you are alive", it is the "attachment of a soul".

Third Eye Control

The third eye name is derived from a little gland in the brain called the pineal "pinecone" gland. The pineal has no apparent use, but it is thought to have been used by our brains at one time. After all, the gland didn't just grow there for no reason, so let's travel back to the Tower of Babel.

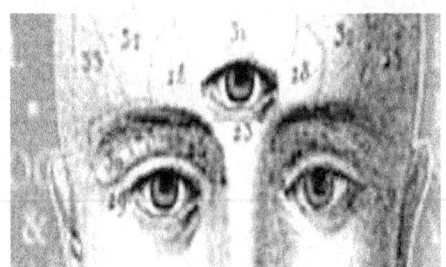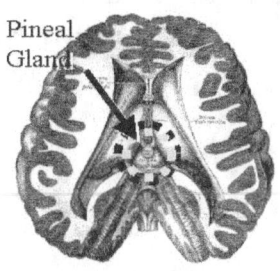

Tower of Babel and the Bharata War

Most of you know something about this huge Tower that King Nimrod had built about 6 thousand years ago, but many may not know about the huge wars that were written about during this time and how 1/3 of all the people on earth were killed as a result of this war. Called the Bharata War in India with the ending called Zep-Tepi [new beginning] by the Egyptians, we know this was a horrible time on the earth. Not to belabor this, let me briefly go into what happened when the Tower of Babel was destroyed thousands of years ago here and how our brains lost most of their capability to understand our soul according to many ancient texts and how this brain loss was probably from some DNA mutations. One of the changes could very well have been a massive reduction in the size and capability of this unusual portion of our brain. For this we need to look at haplotyping.

Haplotyping

Those studying DNA mutation [Haplotyping Science] tells us that there were 2 major massive mutation times in human existence. The first was 11 thousand years ago just before the Pleistocene Extinction and Worldwide flood of that time. The second was about 55 hundred years ago which corresponds to this horrible war. A typical Haplotype/Mutation map is shown next. The D, DE, E, F, G, H, I, J, T, and K mutations all occurred about 11 thousand years ago while the L, M, N, O, P, Q, R, and S mutations seem to have happened around the end of the Bharata War.

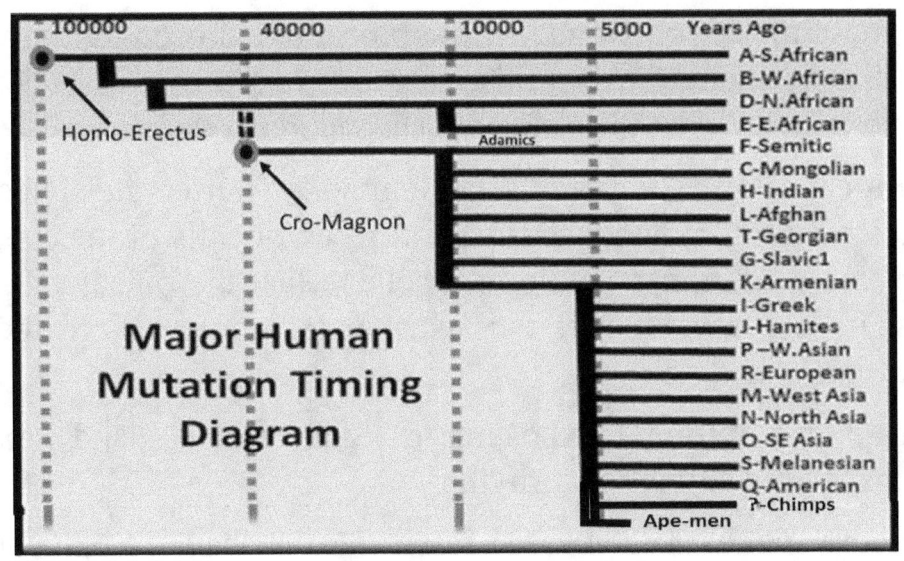

Major Human Mutation Timing Diagram

Atrophied Brain

I must bring out the unusual fact that our current brain size is smaller than our earlier cousins, Neanderthal. While that fact is well known, what is not recognized is that this reduction in brain size shows that our brains began atrophying from disuse about 6 thousand years ago. I could bring out the fact that the entire world was plunged into some type of Stone Age re-insurgence 5 to 6 thousand years ago and people seemed to become dumb as stumps for a while. The Biblical book of Jasher simply tells us that 1/3 of the people died, <u>1/3 of the people became like apes</u> and 1/3 of the people were dispersed to places around the world because they could only talk to their close relatives. The PreMaya indicated that they lost many other abilities. We can imagine that before this brain reduction occurred, we could do many things with our bigger brain we cannot do today. We can imagine that the pineal gland, prior to whatever happened 6 thousand years ago also was larger and might have been used by our ancestors. I could also bring up many other things that would make you wonder if the pineal gland used to allow us to do many things in the past, but I won't. Instead, let me tell you what this tiny, pea-shaped gland does.

Pineal Glands in many non-mammalian vertebrates have a strong resemblance to the photoreceptor cells of the eye. Some evolutionary biologists believe that the pineal cells share a common were the ancestor to retina cells in the eye.

In some animals exposure to light of this gland can change the animal's biorhythm.

Some early vertebrate fossil skulls have a pineal opening so that it probably had some vision characteristic.

The lamprey and the tuatara both have this same type of pineal opening and this thing is photosensitive. The structures appear to include cornea, lens and retina,

The pineal gland is weird in that it <u>has profuse blood flow, second only to the kidney</u>, so we can be sure that it once was of great importance. While doctors are perplexed at why this insignificant gland would need so much blood, it is obvious that whatever happened 6 thousand years ago made the extra blood flow unnecessary.

The brain of a 90 million year old bird was found with a large parietal eye and pineal gland so it's been used for some time now to provide additional insight beyond normal seeing.

Fluoride and HGH Disaster

One of the worse issues in finding happiness is gender questioning disorders like homosexuality, bestiality, Transgenderism, Necrophilia, and all the rest. These issues start in children who become too sexually aware too soon and cannot process pheromone response properly or some trauma initiates a bizarre response. Today we are finding that the pineal might be involved.

Production of melatonin by the pineal gland is stimulated by darkness and inhibited by light. This melatonin stuff affects sex drive. Today scientists are finding massive amounts of fluoride in and around this gland, at least in environments that allow for too much fluorine entrance. Since fluoride infusion into our water happened about the same time as the huge expansion of children being uncertain about their sexual role, some believe that the underage sex drive may be responsible for the increase in sexual deviation we are seeing. Fear got so bad that Teflon coated frying pans were pretty much taken off the market as the fluorine came off when scratched. To be fair, just as many are saying pregnant women and small children who are allowed to and do eat Human Growth Hormone [HGH] in beef also add to this dilemma as small girls are now growing breasts and menstruating too soon showing too strong a sexual drive.

One possible way to increase happiness is to stop eating HGH infused meat and switch to ceramic frying pans.

OK! We have a tiny organ that used to be huge and it used to be an aid in seeing, regulating moods and sex drive, but our bodies are still trying to supply it with enough blood to run a huge organ. Today the tiny little thing seems to have been abandoned by our bodies except for the sex thing, but maybe we just can't see what it can do without vibrating a little. Vibrating allows us to understand our world. Possibly, before the Bharata war we had the ability to speak with few words as indicated in the Bible [telepathy], we could sense things at long distances [astral-projection], and we could control our environment as the PreMaya told us. We can imagine that going outside the confines of our normal reality was commonplace. Possibly everyone could walk across water. One thing we know is that the Tower of Babel has some of the largest building blocks ever produced by man weighing over 3 million pounds each. As we have no equipment today that can carry these things to the Babel citadel in Lebanon [Baalbek], one might wonder just who carried them and how. A couple of images are shown next. The first is of one stone that has been completely finished and in on the ground many miles from the citadel. The tiny person on top is a "normal guy. The second image is of a guy standing next to some of the remains. If you look closely you will see the first 3 rows of the sight are what we could say are normal huge blocks, while the next two layers have stones so huge you cannot image the size. The stones above this level were "replaced" by the Romans as this whole sight had been smashed just like the Babel story in the Bible indicated. The circle shows where a normal size guy is standing. So here is the dilemma. When that was being made, it was so easy to move these massive things, they didn't even put them on the bottom. If you are thinking levitation was normal to them, I'm with you.

The following images show that thee huge stones are found everywhere as they seems to have been thrown from the main citadel during some massive cataclysm. Each of the following 6 stones has a person in the picture.

Without this pineal thing, it may be harder to accomplish these things, but true happiness requires us to focus on our soul entity, channel our energy away from Sex, Self, and survival long enough to capture the wonders of "true" life. We can believe these people were pretty happy as they could certainly control their environment. If we travel to the other side of the world, the PreMaya tell us about this wonderful time. The excerpt comes from the *Popul Vuh*, their holy book.

- *They [The people before the famous Mayan calendar was started in 3100BC], had the power of understanding; they saw and could immediately see far* [Wisdom beyond anything possible by the time of this writing. We can believe these people could do unbelievable things as they controlled their reality.]

- *They succeeded in knowing everything that could be seen or known in the world.* [Beyond what we consider real]

- *Things that were hidden in the distance they could see without moving first.* [Seems to reference some ability for out-of-body movement]

- *Their wisdom was great; they controlled the forests, the rocks, the lakes, the seas and the valleys.* [Jesus told his disciples with faith of a grain of mustard seed anyone could do this.]

- *They investigated the four corners of the earth,* [Possibly in flying machines or some other fast transport that needed no machine]

- *They investigated the four corners of heaven.* [Somehow they visited outer space, either in the body or out of it.]

- *They investigated the round surface of the earth.* [They circumnavigated the globe.]

After explaining the capabilities of the Aztalaneans or PreMaya, the texts then goes on to tell about what happened after the famous "Tower of Babel debacle".

- *Then one day the heart of heaven blew fog in their eyes,* [People lost the capability of easily do the seemingly impossible.]

- *They could not see clearly any more, like breathing on a mirror.* [They lost their wisdom]

- *Their eyes were covered and they could only see things that were nearby.*

- *This was the way that the wisdom and knowledge of these first people was destroyed.* [In Jewish version of the Babel War, some of the survivors were turned into ape-men. Just like the Jewish version the Aztalaneans survivors of the War lost the ancient wisdom of people around the world.]

We can believe the PreMaya were very happy and had a larger pineal gland. If we could grow our gland back we could gain a higher level of happiness.

Abraham Maslow Again

Anyway! This pineal gland/third eye was supposed to have given us the ability to understand the reality around us. If we increase our vibrational level by unison with our environment "some call it meditation" or by other exotic means, we can sometimes get in tune with the world around us and here is the odd part. We can even affect it. Another way of saying this is that the 3rd eye thing is that "Self–Actualization" that Abraham Maslow talked about.

Self-Actualization using the Third Eye increases you true happiness.

Positive Thinking-Somehow getting our vibrational levels in tune with the vibrational patterns of the elements around us allows us to be more intuitive. We can sense reactions needed to affect the environment. As we affect the environment we can change it. Now the changes are extremely subtle. You cannot, for instance cause money to fly off a tree, but you can somehow affect the conditions around you that will make it easier to accomplish particular tasks simply by concentrating on these tasks and believing that these things will be accomplished. I know it sounds like gobbly-gook. The problem is that the affect is demonstrated over and over and over again. Positive thinking and getting in tune with the vibrational pattern of the environment actually works. There is no doubt about it. The issue is trying to get into the level of consciousness needed to get the universe to "Bend" a little is not only hard, it also is not easily sustained once one gets to this level of consciousness. As we raise our awareness of self, we lose the ability to manipulate an interface between our self and the rest of the universe. With this knowledge we can see a "chakra level" is simply a vibrational frequency of the conscious. As the frequency increases, the amount we can affect the "life force" increases as well.

A Third Eye Explanation

Noted Near death researcher, Dr. Schofield, came up with a very good description of what or who the people are that "help us" whenever we get into the highest level of consciousness. He described it in 2 dimensions so even I could understand. In his explanation, he presented people that lived in a 2-dimension world. Someone from a 3-dimensional world tries to show them a sphere. It was believed that the sphere could allow a better communication between the two-dimensional beings, it could expand the awareness of the 2-dimensional guys, and it would explain the greater reality. For the two-dimensional being there was simply no way to view the sphere. In their world, it always looked like a circle. No matter how much the 3-dimensional people tried to explain the sphere, the more confused the 2-dimension people got, but the 3-dimensional beings kept on trying to enhance to advance in personal understanding, by means of communication and providing a feeling of joy to the 2-dimensional people. After a while, some understanding of the unbelievable could take place.

Vibration and Conscious Beings-It would seem that there may be people that are sort of suspended in some type of in-between-land that can be seen and communicated with whenever one is vibrated to the Crown Consciousness level. Unfortunately, I cannot give you a very good explanation of this. My very dear friend, Ed Kaprock [This isn't his real name so don't even try to pry it out of me.] however, believes he has been able to achieve this level of consciousness a number of times and believes that the people we see in this altered state can be considered to be teachers. Here is the problem. The teachers try to explain the things that you cannot understand at this level of understanding because you try to relate everything to our normal sensations excited by the workings of our universe. He tells me that over many "trips" to communicate with these people, they have allowed him to see things in a different light. He now feels that he is much more in tune with the consciousness around us and that he cannot completely explain the difference. My friend is almost always at ease and happy in his attempts at expanding his awareness, but let me put out this warning. If you somehow get to a point where you can see these "teachers", question yourself. Do I always get answers I like? If so I would say these are demonic images and could cause ultimate harm.

Before we can get to the "transfer or spirit dimensional quality, we still have one more chakra level we must explore and this is a wild one. We can say this crown chakra certainly will enhance you happiness, but it is truly weird.

Crown Consciousness

According to Buddhists the highest vibrational Chakra is the Crown. As people expand their awareness more and more or become more self-actualized, as Maslow said, we become more and more <u>conscious of other worlds</u> or universes. Our conscious becomes more in tune with other universes because they are an integral part of this universe. Guess how people describe how to change to higher and higher chakras. They indicate that each expansion is like <u>a vibrational realization</u>. The more the realization or level of chakra becomes; <u>the more noticeable is this strange vibration.</u> The method for getting to this "crown" thing is to sort of hypnotize yourself. "Relax! You are getting sleepy! You are completely unaware of your surroundings! You feel a warmness and a sense of comfort! Wait just a minute! I'm getting numb here and I can't do the crown chakra dance right now. I have to continue writing this book.

We are told if you get near this state, the body will begin to hum and vibrate in a low comforting tone and it almost warms your entire body and your feet and hands seem to disappear. Wow! The first time it happens, the sense of comfort is great but nothing more may have happened. A second and third time might be tried and the world around you is forgotten as you slide into the vibrational level associated with the crown chakra. Vibration, vibration,

vibration- if that isn't the weirdest thing I ever heard. Hold on just one minute, vibrations are not odd in this book. Vibration frequencies define how a person perceives this universe just like the vibrating fermion that begins to perceive the other particles around it. Let's think of this whole consciousness a little. Let me start over with a question.

Can your consciousness REALLY leave your body?

I'm sure your first thought is that it can't but don't be so ready to close your mind to things that seem to be going on around us. It is becoming more and more apparent each year that astral projection, near death experiences, seers getting their prophesies, and even reincarnations have been and are elements of the same characterization of the consciousness dimension. I know you think you are using your consciousness right now, but there is more to it that you would like to believe. Let me give you a few examples.

Near Death Experiences

It is believed that over 10 million Americans have had Near Death Experiences and lived to tell about it.

One need only go to the near death experience website and find 2000 verified or at least printed events involving near death experiences both good and bad. The website is [http://www.nderf.org] for those interested in a first glimpse. Below is a common theme in just about all of these things.

- *It is said that the soul [I call it sub consciousness, but some like to separate us a little more.] goes through this tunnel like "Whoosh".*

- *After the whoosh feeling you are standing in the brightest white light you have ever known. The noonday sun cannot compare to its brightness or stark whiteness.*

- *You instantly feel this bright white light raining down upon your spirit.*

- *You feel an intense love all over your body like soft rain falling on your skin. You know you are loved beyond all shadow of a doubt by this bright whiteness surrounding your spirit.*

- *You feel totally at peace and very safe and love is in you and around everywhere.*

- *You would be typically calm and have no real thought of whatever had "almost" killed you, no pain just absolute peace.*

- *It is said that you feel odd about still thinking, and how alert you are.*

- *Someone may ask, "Do you want to stay or do you want to go back?"*

Here is an interesting thing. After this experience, many fell intense happiness and cannot stop helping others well away from the common association with the baser self.

Out Of Body Experiences

If we were just looking at out-of-body experiences in general we would find that they are much more common that we would initially believe. This thing occurs in about 1/4 to 1/3 of the population depending on which study you look at. It would be ludicrous to say that up to one third of the human population are mental illness deviants, when in fact, this is such a common phenomenon. They leave their bodies. They see things at great distances from where their body is. They talk to "friendly and informative" people. They insist that the time they are away is not dreamlike, but instead it is close to reality. They usually sense power and freedom. These people recognize and describe objects seen in these states with great accuracy. Others, including many who initially were very skeptical, have verified this strange fact.

Astral Projection-One type of out-of-body experience is called astral projection. Below is a common projection memory.

- *Over several days a possible projector may try to focus on some special place.*

- *Many concentrate on a mantra [some special relaxation word, phrase, or image] prior when falling asleep.*

- *The mantra is used to sort of allow fast self-hypnosis or allow the body to fall asleep faster.*

- *A mantra is said to also help a person stay conscious enough while in a dream state to have control to some level.*

- *The person would feel their physical body fall asleep while the image of an astral body would emerge and start to rise.*

- *The astral body could go up and out of the experimenter's body.*

- *This is usually easier when the goal was clear.*

- *One can usually feel themselves flying through the air.*

- *As with other out-of-body experiences, sometimes other people can be seen or even talked to during one's travels.*

- *It is said that caution must always be used not to fall into deep dream state at this point.*

- *Many not only view remote sites, but they feel like they gained some personal teaching that stays them in a strong way after the experience.*

Reportedly they, "the travelers", generally, feel at peace when they return to their body.

Common Thread of Happiness

Hopefully, you are seeing that in almost all cases, people begin these experiences by blocking out the world including all feeling. Those who are forced in that condition by some tragedy don't seem to have any difference in this effect. They leave their bodies, get happiness, wisdom, sort of talk to comforting people, get a heightened sense of reality, can float, and when they get focused back on the "real world" they are plummeted back into it. Many times these people are changed forever. The trip to the Crown chakra has changed them forever and I'll tell you why. Their consciousness has been vibrationally enhanced. It vibrates closer to the level needed to do this transfer thing, but in the mean time they become more aware of the feelings of others and become more self-actualized.

These people appeared to be much Happier.

Whether the "people they interact with are the cause of the vibrational enhancement or some other mechanism is at work, I do not know, but the entire life force of the person is enhanced. Many like it so much they go off and do it again if they can. Prophets and seers seem to do it a little differently, but it seems that they get so much enjoyment, they keep on doing it over and over and over.

Prophet Happiness

Something that is similar to astral projection seems to be the ability to tell the future. For that discussion I will bring out some details of Dr. Edgar Casey, and others. While it seems that the seers do leave their body, there is a substantial shift in what happens. Like other out-of-body experiences the seer must generally forget the details of this world. Some of these guys got to the "Crown Consciousness" by going on long fastings. It should be noted that fasting seems to be a major step in attaining higher vibrational resonance and practiced not only by this set of individuals, but also we find the Buddhists, Taoists and others. Another way of separating from this world was done by Nostradamus. He stared into a pool of water for long periods of time. The more they separated themselves, the faster and more accurate were the prophecies. While in this altered state, the seers are somehow given the information. They actually witness the events that would happen in our future. There is one likely reason that Nostradamus, Mother Shipton, John, and Daniel from the Bible and many others all saw and described the future. That reason is BECAUSE the future had already happened at the location that had "projected" themselves to. Somehow this times travel has something to do with happiness, but let's just look at some or the evidence of time travel from a few of these guys. The reason these people are good examples is that after doing this a number of times, it consumed them they LOVED doing this and continued over and over. Even after Mother Shipton learned of her own death she continued to get into a state that separated her from this world so she could view the future.

One way to aid in True happiness is to separate yourself from "reality" and go beyond "reality".

Dr. Casey's Time Travel

Dr. Edgar Casey simply fell asleep to get his answers. While he was in his "trance" he could answer just about any question from medical miracles to future events. For years he was able to amaze, comfort, heal, instruct and help others simply by leaving his body for a while and getting answers from "somewhere else. I don't know if he feel though a tunnel and came to a bright light or any of that, but he did see the future. It is obvious he didn't understand some of the things he saw, but there is enough details in his ramblings that let us know he truly saw the future well before it happened in this universe. Some of his predictions have come true and some still wait as indicated below

The Stock Market Crash *of 1929 was foretold in February 1925.*

In 1935, Edgar Cayce warned of World War II *calling the Germans the Aryan race.*

The Beginning of the Earth's Poles shifting *was predicted in 1936. He actually indicated that the shift would begin around 2000 to 2001AD. Sure enough we now know the shifting has begun.*

Convergence of Communications Companies *was predicted in 1929 and seen "Ma Bell began its quest about 5 years following the prediction.*

The Dead Sea Scrolls *were predicted as Edgar Cayce mentioned the Essene 10 years before the Dead Sea Scrolls were discovered in 1947.*

Blood was predicted to become a Diagnostic Tool. *He knew it would happen in 1927.*

La Niña and El Niño Effects were explained. *Amazingly, on May 28, 1926, Edgar Cayce connected the temperature changes in deep ocean currents to weather changes in the United States. I know it sounds ridiculous, but that is what he predicted.*

Some of his predictions have not happened yet, but things seem to be looking more like the descriptions of this unusual guy.

In 1926, he predicted that our life-spans would extend. *I know we are still struggling, but with all the body parts being cloned and gene splicing, the ravages of time will soon be lessened. None of that was happening in 1926.*

 He predicted that we will discover the design for a self-fueling perpetual-motion machine. *Many designs are almost there today.*

In 1941 he predicted a major conflict in the Persian Gulf. *He actually indicated that the areas to look for would be Libya, Egypt, Ankara, in Syria, and in the Persian Gulf."*

We will gain expanding consciousness was predicted in 1942, He said that individual had to essentially work with personal soul development in order to **_resonate_** to that new consciousness: This gives us insight into the method for gaining insight. He would somehow allow his body or soul to vibrate to a higher level just like many are now trying to indicate [Besides, it goes along with my book.].

In 1932 he indicated that an ancient "Hall of Records" would be discovered in Egypt. He said that the people of Atlantis became aware of the fact that their civilization was about to be destroyed. As a result, they hid identical records of the Atlantean civilization in Bimini, in Egypt and in the Yucatan. The records contain a record of Atlantis from the beginnings of those periods when the Spirit took form, the first destruction and the changes that took place in the land. He even identified exactly where. He said that it is located where the sun rises from the waters, the line of the shadow falls between the paws of the Sphinx.

He told us about China become a world power. He said that eventually China would become "the cradle of Christianity, as applied in the lives of men and that it would take a long time to manifest but that it was the country's destiny.

He prophesied about the Second Coming of God. He not only told us a lot about the "missing" years of Jesus' He indicated that the time and half time has been fulfilled in this day the Lord, will come, even as they had have seen him go. I know he could have looked in "Revelation", but it did give us an indication of his Christian faith.

Mother Shipton's Time Travel

Let me reintroduce Mother Shipton for those that don't recognize the name. Her real name was Ursula Sontheil. Her last name was hard to pronounce so she married a guy named Toby Shipton. Now Ursula was not pretty at all. Warts and all the witch-like looks were indicated in documents and drawings so people believed she put a spell on old Toby. After he died, she became more recluse than she normally was and she started living in the future so to speak. She wrote cute poems around her predictions, but they are interesting in their own rite. We don't have details about how she vibrated into a new level of consciousness, but we do know some of the things she saw. Let me share one of Mother Shipton's visions about a new queen that would come to the throne only 3 years before Ursula was burned to death. You will notice Queen Elizabeth I, Francis Drake, The defeat of the Spanish Armada and other things she simply could not have known about as they occurred after she had died.

The Maiden Queen full many a year- Shall England's warlike scepter bear. Those who sighed, then shall sing- And the bells shall changes ring. The Papal Power shall bear no sway. & Rome's trash shall hence be swept away. The locusts from the 7 hills This English Rose shall seek to kill- & the Western monarch's wooden horses -shall be destroyed by Drake's forces.

Besides her own awful death, she predicted the following:

- *The rise of the Church of England*

- *The California gold rush*

- *Automobiles,* *Radios,* *telephones,* *telegraphs,* *hydroelectric power-*

- *Manufacture of mountain tunnels* and *Commercial air travel*

- ***Submarines,*** *airplanes, iron ships, & airborne military and their use-*

- ***World War I***, *US Civil War, and the French Revolution-*

- ***British and French alliance*** *during World War I and II-*

- ***The Allies and Communist*** *bloc, and the cold War-*

- ***The France to England*** *underwater tunnel-*

- ***Women would commonly wear pants*** *and have short hair, [an unthinkable thing at the time. OK Ursula thought it, but she still wore the huge pile of clothes that every other woman wore.]*

- ***The printing press*** *and how it would change writing*

- ***She saw the coming of a comet*** *that will sort-of begin the spiral downhill for mankind.*

- ***After the comet Mother Shipton saw war***, *famine, tyrannical rule, the tribulation period and finally a long lasting peace just before the eventual end. [This was very similar to one of her contemporaries named Nostradamus and the marvelous revelation of John in the Bible as well as some of the details in the predictions made by George Washington when he was given his viewing of the future and wrote down the fearful details.*

Let's look at some of these insights! In her predictions she used the year 1926 as a base and continued from there. I don't know why, but that's what I read. By that time, the following will occur in the next 25 years.

For those who live the century through - in fear and trembling this shall do. "Flee to the mountains and the dens -to bog and forest and wild fens. For storms will rage and oceans roar when Gabriel stands on sea and shore, and as he blows his wondrous horn old worlds die and new be born.

The catastrophe above will happen just before the year 2026, and she goes on to explain just how the earth dies and is reborn. Let me go over the dies part. The reborn part you can find in some of the 2012 novels.

God's messenger from the heavens (comet) arrives and a great sound is heard as it passes through Earth's atmosphere and impacts Earth. It causes wild storms and raging seas. A fiery dragon will cross the sky six times before the earth shall die. Mankind will tremble and frightened be for the six heralds in this prophecy.

A comet' tail could, very well be considered a "dragon tail". The prediction could mean six major meteor strikes will occur which are spawned by the comet strike. It could also mean that before a terrible comet strike, we one earth will witness the huge ball of material getting closer and closer for 6 days before the eventual impact. Either way there is some bad stuff coming.

For seven days and seven nights man will watch this awesome sight. The tides will rise beyond their ken. To bite away the shores and then mountains will begin to roar and earthquakes split the plain to shore. And flooding waters rushing in will flood the lands with such a din that mankind cowers in muddy fen and snarls about his fellow men. He bares his teeth and fights and kills and secrets food in secret hills and ugly in his fear, he lies to kill marauders, thieves and spies.

This comet strike evidently happens over a seven-day period or on the 7th day. One of the major issues of this event is worldwide flooding. Like the web-bot's prediction of Florida and other low-lying places will be underwater around the year 2009 and Dr. Casey's prediction that soon, the two halves of the United States will be split apart, these words are ominous and people begin killing each other over food.

The world upside down shall be, and gold found at the root of a tree. Yet greater sign there be to see as man nears latter century. Three sleeping mountains gather breath- spew out mud, ice and earth and earthquakes swallow town and town. Not every soul on earth will die, as the dragon's tail [Comet] goes sweeping by, not every land on earth will sink, but these will wallow in stench and stink of rotting bodies of beast and man, of vegetation crisped on land.

This seems to be saying that the Earth axis will shift either before or after the comet strike. It is not known when. Her centuries ended on the 26th year after a normal turn of the century, so she was talking about the time between 2001 and 2026. Earthquake and Volcanic action becomes significant. Both could be caused by the comet or by the upcoming Earth axis shift.

Then shall be the Son of Man, having a fierce beast in his arms, whose kingdom is the land of the moon, which is dreaded throughout the world. Man flees in terror from the flood and kills, and rapes and lies in blood and spilling blood by mankind's hands will stain and bitter many lands. And when the dragon's tail [comet] is gone man forgets and smiles and carries on. To apply himself too late, too late for mankind has earned deserved fate.

After the comet, blood is spilled by war. Oddly, this includes war in space. Now, I have no idea where Mother Shipton could have gotten the space angle unless she actually saw it. The reference to the moon seems to be referencing involvement with others from outside the earth. The son of man in this verse is not a reference to God's son, but is, evidently, the leader of the "Christian Nations". He has a secret alliance with this beast thing. By using this alliance, he begins to take power away from the Moslem horde. Apparently, this beast he has in his arms, we can imagine that this has to do with the Biblical "mark of the beast" that will BECOME dread throughout the world.

Muslim War

War will follow with the work in the land of the Pagan and Turk The lily [USA?] shall be moved against the seed of the lion [Persia], and shall stand on one side of the country with a number of ships. <u>With a number</u> shall he pass many waters and shall come to the land of the lion [Persia], looking for help from the beast of his country <u>The lily F.K. shall lose his crown</u>, and therewith be crowned the Son of Man K.W. and the fourth year shall be preferred.

This seems to indicate that the Turks will eventually follow the Moslem nations in this pre-Tribulation War. "Lily to the rescue": the Moslem lion is beaten back by a nation with a strong Navy, possibly USA. Then some group goes a great distance across the water, probably the

USA, to fight the Moslem Lion. Unknown to them, they will be aided by the beast or what Nostradamus called the Prince of Hell. Evidently the United States "Lily" and the Son of Man "Prince of Hell" rule the world together for a time, but the old Prince takes full control after 4 years. Shipton even told us something about them with the peculiar initials. If someone becomes president with the initials FK I'm going to start worrying. Mother Shipton went on and on about how the world would be, not because she simply knew it or dreamed about it. She actually saw what was going to happen, by all accounts. Naturally she could not understand all of what she saw, so there are limitations to what we can get from the sightings, but it is fairly apparent that all that will happen has already happened "somewhere".

The reason these "seers kept on separating themselves from society and doing these things must be that they gain substantial happiness.

Nostradamus and John

Both Nostradamus and the Revelation of John in the Bible both parallel the prophesies of Mother Shipton. Nostradamus who was a contemporary of Mother Shipton also foretold the collapse of the twin towers in 2011 and provides us with a large amount of data concerning the Moslem War to come, but there can be little doubt that all three saw the same future. As I will explain later, this crown vibration level seems to allow for the transfer between our universe and the one typically called heaven that is linked to this one so let's look at this interesting level of consciousness. From here let me give you a snapshot into the Spirit part of "you". What we find is the spirit part of you is so removed from "reality" it has no position concerning happiness or sadness.

Your Spirit

I mentioned this Spirit portion of your life and completely ignored it as we discussed various elements of true Happiness, but in some ways, the Spirit is the ultimate element of true happiness. You plowed through <u>"Life"</u> as a dimensional quality needed to experience this thing we call reality. Probably, you became cautious with the whole concept of <u>"Consciousness"</u> being a dimension and required for the universe to exist, but now I have just gone too far with something that is pretty weird. [OK! A lot of this is weird; but a Spirit gave this weirdness to us.] I won't be able to present a very good level of explanation for this very confusing component of living, because it has to do with soul transfer between universes and I can't find anyone to give me concrete answers about how it all works. Instead, I am going to give you general descriptions of the spirit.

Make no mistake, the spirit is a dimensional quality required part for the life, death and existence of those who affect our universe, so do not simply ignore it.

One thing we know. All dimensional elements of our reality have a level of similarity and interaction. It must be that way or they would not be all part of our universal building blocks. From the similar elements of matter and force we can believe that we gain more spiritual energy as we increase our vibrational frequency.

Let me tell you this as a truth. Trying to put definitions around this "thing" is difficult. It has no mass and no motion so it isn't associated with either matter or photonic forces. That doesn't mean that we cannot "connect with our linked universe. This one may be the most important connection dimension we will ever understand. What I call the "Spirit" is the connective component of the life. We are told it is, sort of, a key or gateway for living things between this universe and another. According to the Biblical testimony, the "LIGHT" [Spirit of life] was brought into the world ages before the sun became a beacon in the sky.

Genesis 1:1-3: *In the beginning God created the heavens and the earth. Now the earth became formless and empty, darkness was over the surface of the deep, and the Spirit of God was hovering over the waters. And God said, "Let there be light," and there was light. God called the light "day," and the darkness he called "night." And there was evening, and there was morning—**the first AGE.***

Many claimed foul and say the Bible is a lie as "light" without a sun makes no sense as we were told three Ages Later---

Genesis 1:15-19- *God made two great lights—the greater light to govern the day and the lesser light to govern the night. He also made the stars. God set them in the vault of the sky to give light on the earth, to govern the day and the night, and to separate light from darkness. And God saw* *that it was good. And there was evening, and there was morning—**the fourth AGE**.*

Today we know that light with a sun and no cognizant viewer makes no sense. Moses' writings here were possibly the very first introduction into Anthropics science ever recorded.

This "light", as we later find out, is the transfer key to a linked universe. Just like going through a black hole if you are matter or a magnetic monopole if you are energy, the spirit or "light" transfers the released soul.

The Genesis story continues as this "light" was taken away from people before the end of the Pleistocene extinction and worldwide flood. Evidently, this "light" was in the early, Chosen People, survivors [Noah and his family]. With this "spirit", one could or can enter into a new universe called "Heaven". It was and is an extension of our life-consciousness beyond our death. Let me provide you with a few of the references that can be found about this mysterious "Light" and then we will discuss how or why we must consider it as you try to experience true happiness. Remember you can substitute spirit for light if you want to. The early Jews had no word for this thing so "Light" had to do.

Jubilees

The book of Jubilees is still considered a canon book of the Bible by some Christian sects. It contains many similar stories to our current Bible including stories about a strange thing called the "Light". This is talking about the Anak people who had been punished by God by removing this "Light thing".

133

Jubilees 2:9- *Nor may we [The Anak people] take revenge on him because he has stripped us of the* <u>*"light"*</u> *[remember to substitute spirit]. God marked out the borders of the world and created man in his own image with whom he hopes* <u>*again*</u> *to populate heaven, with pure souls.* [Not only note that without this light thing, the Anak could not take vengeance on any of the heavenly host. They lost some substantial power. Also note that the word "again" is put in the verse to let us know that Anak people originally came from this linked universe [They had been people].

Please notice that this light [spirit] was required to allow SOULS to enter into the Heaven universe. One could say that is the ultimate happiness.

I John

In the New Testament, the "light" continued as a connection between this world and the next. In this case, the word light had no sunlight meaning. It was talking about the way to heaven.

I John 1:5-7- *God is light, and there is no darkness in him at all. So we are lying if we say we have fellowship with God but go on living in* **spiritual darkness***;* [From this we find that we sort of have a weak spirit that needs to be energized to get it away from what they called spiritual darkness. We can substitute darkness for sadness and the light then would be spirit happiness.]

Spiritual Happiness is a very important type of happiness.

Mishaf Resh

This verse comes from the Zoroastrian religion. This verse about the strange "Light" thing comes from their version of their Holy Bible called Mishaf Resh. *Before the creation of heaven and earth Gad dwelt upon the sea. Then God went up to Heaven and solidified it. Out of His essence and light he made six gods.* [Like the others, this was not talking about sunlight. Instead it was talking about the Spirit part of life. Also the 6 gods were really 6 archangels so don't worry about this strange religion.]

Zadspram

The Zoroastrian religion began around 700 BC, so it's been around a while. In the book Zadspram we find the "Light" thing again. *From the seed which was the ox's, they would carry off from it and the "light" was entrusted to the angel of the moon in a special place, the seed was thoroughly purified by the "light" and was restored in its many qualities.* [OK, the Zoroastrians had a higher feeling about animals, but the Light here is, again, the spirit. Please note that in our religion, the Holy Spirit expands the normal capabilities of a person's "normal" spirit. The Holy Spirit restored many important "qualities".]

Emerald Texts

This comes from ancient Egypt; it was, presumably, written by King Thoth, who was the ruler during the Bharata War 6 thousand years ago. *The Children of Light dwelt among us* [Please note the "Light" description as the soul somehow can be connected with this "light" or spirit after death. *---the children of light are different when they are not incarnate in a physical body".* Thirty-Two *were there of the children of the sons of light who had come among men.* [According to this book, only 32 of the sons of this "light" survived the Pleistocene Extinction and worldwide flood. Jewish history suggested only 8 individuals with the "light" survived among there group.]

Maori Tradition

According to the Maori tradition, a **huge war of the gods** *followed the separation of the earth and heaven. After a 2nd war in heaven, God forced rebels to other worlds of darkness and despair* [The earth became desolate just like the Genesis story]. *God forced the sky away from the Earth and Light came into existence.* [Notice again that light had nothing to do with the sun. It seemed to only be needed when Heaven and earth were separated--- It was like a key to go between them.]

While these don't help too much in our search for the details concerning how this SPIRIT/light can enhance our happiness, the New Testament may help a little more as spiritual happiness is just as important and you soul happiness which is infinitely more important than the "Self" happiness.

New Testament Spirit

Typically, in the New Testament of our Bible, we find more pointed information about this light than provided in the book of "I John". Instead of being called "Light" this transfer part of our life is simply called the Holy Spirit. Jesus indicated that he left the Holy Spirit to "fill" those on the earth or bring Light" to our spirit so we can transfer to the Heaven universe. It's the same thing as this "Light" that is being talked about by all these other writers. They simply didn't know to call it the Holy Spirit. We are told our "Spirit, without the "Holy Spirit" is the Spirit of Darkness. Possibly we can talk about the Holy Spirit simply being a flashlight for the spirit.

Almost Absent From The Body

Dying is really what really can get the soul going.

Did you remember the thief on the cross next to the dying Jesus was promised that *the day he died, he would be with Jesus in paradise.* It sounds like the souls leave this universe, but that does not mean that his soul immediately left this world and went to heaven. Remember that Jesus didn't even go to heaven for days after he died. If you remember in the Old Testament when Saul asked the witch of Endor to let him talk to Samuel, that she conjured away and the dead prophet, Samuel, woke up to tell Saul that he and both his sons would be slaughtered in an upcoming battle. Samuel's soul was not in heaven. In the New Testament many instances of demons were discussed where these demons could possess bodies and they were made to leave by Jesus and others. From what we can imagine, the countless people, in the New Testament, who were brought back to life when they had died had never ventured into Heaven and could tell no one what had happened to them. When a boy's dead body touched the bones of Elisha, he came back to life and knew nothing about any heavenly or hellish place. On and on we could go to show that when people die, they do not immediately go into heaven. In fact, in the book of Revelation we are told that the "Dead in Christ" will rise out of their graves in the last days. The reason the dead rise is that they are still on the earth. The reason I'm saying all these things is not to make this a Bible class, but to instill the possibility that when you die, your spirit my go to our linked universe, but your <u>soul</u> does not. For what it is worth, let me tell you a possibility concerning the end of days. God incarnate [Jesus} will come back to this world to get his followers. Some are dead and some will be alive, but the souls of all of them will go to Heaven on that day. The method of transfer is what we can call the Spirit dimensional quality of life. Being able to transfer between one universe and the next is a thing of great happiness.

With all this, hopefully you are beginning to understand true happiness is almost the opposite of what you FEEL is happiness or temporary happiness, or emotional comfort. These sweep away the ability for us to help mold our universe, see our maker and transfer to another universe.

Gaining Happiness Overview

As I stated, to gain happiness we must reject those things we had believed to be causing happiness. Instead we must really work at it. Here are some of the ways we discussed that enhance true happiness in our soul.

- *Self-Actualization seems to increase Happiness*

- *Positive thinking increases our happiness.*

- *Visualization of success regardless of a situation increases our happiness.*

- *Increasing our vibrational resonance increase happiness.*

- *Going near the speed of light increases our happiness.*

- *Meditation increases happiness.*

- *Rejecting Self/Sex/Survival increases our happiness.*

- *Seeing the Future increases happiness.*

- *Having a larger Pineal Gland seems to increase happiness.*

- *Faith increases happiness.*

- *Faith in God increase happiness even more.*

- *Adding the "light" to our spirit increases happiness.*

- *Astral projection seems to increase happiness.*

- *Near death experiences increases happiness.*

- *Your brain sensing ultra-low frequencies seems to enhance happiness.*

- *Releasing your soul in death makes the Soul happiness increase.*

Surprisingly, things we thought would make us feel happy do the opposite. These include things like:

- *Having sex with a beautiful woman.*

- *Eating a triple steak burger with cheese and French fries*

- *The pride you feel from lifting more weight than others around you.*

- *Lazing around on a Saturday morning.*

- *Getting gifts on you Birthday.*

- *The surge of power filling you after defeating your enemy.*

All these things sound like you would gain happiness, but we find that to be fleeting. It drives your senses back into the lowest regions of self/sex/and survival and those around us will be pulled down as well. I know this doesn't make sense. You say after sex I always feel good, but the sensation of orgasm is truly traumatic to your body. The spasms are almost identical to that one would feel from electrocution. The sluggishness from overeating pushes our bodies into misery, and lazy begets lazier. Self-centered pride pulls us into ourselves and away for true love as does the momentary feeling of glee when someone buys us something special.

The only reason I'm bringing up instances from Biblical texts is that you can relate to them. When you die, if you soul left this universe, there would have to be another soul entering the universe to allow for the transfer and keep both worlds "Neutral". I know you are going to say a baby gets born, so a soul would have to be transferred by means of the SPIRIT dimension. As the Bible told us souls are not leaving our universe, something else must happen. We can believe a number of released souls are free and either sleeping or active for short periods. <u>Vibrating at the speed of light, time has no meaning to a released soul dimensional quality</u>. If a new Life/self [Baby] is to be established, many times, released souls would "become" these now carnal entities just to make "life" even more confusing. We call this reincarnation.

Reincarnation Happiness?

We have this soul vibrating at the speed of light and no time passes, but he is completely aware of the universe--- well beyond this reality.

Happy Souls

The question is twofold. Are "awake/released souls" happy and when they slow down drastically to become reincarnated are they happy? In both instances the answer is not really. Without a "Self" the soul cannot experience life unless there is an "interface with a "live" entity. As the soul vibration slows down, there would be a level of depression. Haven't you see babies cry?---- That was a joke. A baby has no reference of sad and happy initially.

For detail in reincarnation and bringing forward happiness into a new "self" I will have to expand your knowledge of vibrational matter and symmetry of our linked universes, but on the surface there is a simple supposition. Dead guys [Souls] get tired of being dead and come back. By all accounts, almost always these entries are into babies. The kicker is that many remember something from past lives. Reincarnation is the attachment of a soul or "consciousness" to various living people over time. I know you have heard about Buddhists who believe that people could come back as animals, but that makes no sense. What would our consciousness do in an animal???? Some point to the Bible to gain assurance that reincarnation is an impossible task, but instead, the Bible does identify reincarnation "sort of"----

Hebrews 9:27 -*"For it is appointed for men to die once and after this comes judgment."* [Some indicate that this indicates that a consciousness only lives once because of this verse. It doesn't say that. OK! It does sound like that, but other places seem to point towards a more loose characterization of the Spirit and a released soul.]

John 3:13-<u>No one has ever gone into heaven</u> except the one who came from heaven--the Son of Man. [Please understand what this is saying. I know it is not what some have told you, but <u>NO souls</u> besides those of residents called angels are in heaven. As many have died, either there is a huge pile of released souls or we live more than one carnal adventure to gain happiness.] To make it more plane, Jesus indicated he had to go and prepare a place for them and would come again to take everyone home.

Matthew 11,14 - *"And if you are willing to accept it, John the Baptist is the Elijah who was to come." ---"But I tell you, Elijah has already come, and they did not recognize him, but have done to him everything they wished. In the same way the Son of Man is going to suffer at their hands."* [Certainly if John the Baptist was Elijah, there is something going on that is reincarnation-like.]

Malachi (3:1; 4:5-6)- *"See, I will send you the prophet Elijah before that great and dreadful day of the Lord comes."*

John 9:2 -*"Rabbi, who sinned, this man or his parents, that he was born blind?"* [It is obvious that the first option (the man was born blind because of his sin) implies that he could sin <u>only</u> in a previous life.]

142

1 Corinthians 15:42,43,51,52- Our bodies will be raised "in incorruption, glory and power"--- We shall <u>not all</u> <u>sleep</u>, but we shall all be changed. In a moment, in the twinkling of an eye, at the last trump: for the trumpet shall sound, and the dead shall be raised incorruptible, and we shall be changed [As I mentioned before, there would be no reason for dead rising if their consciousness had already left the earth. I know some have told you that a nasty body that had been in the ground for thousands of years is what is going to rise, but that makes no sense. Also there is a reason why Paul indicated, "Not all sleep." That, simply, is that most people "sleep" after they die. Some sleep for many years. People don't go to heaven until the end of days. While they are on earth we can imagine that they either sleep or go to other bodies. Just how many billions of people have been on the earth from 40 thousand years ago until now anyway?]

1Thessalonians 4:15-17- For the Lord himself will come down from heaven, with a loud command, with the voice of the archangel and with the trumpet call of God, and <u>the dead in Christ will rise first</u>. After that, we who are still alive and are left will be caught up together with them in the clouds to meet the Lord in the air. And so we will be with the Lord forever. [Again the dead people don't leave the earth until the last days so they are somewhere on the earth right now if all of them were ghosts, No one would want to buy a house or sleep with a light off or anything like that. Everything would be haunted by now if it weren't for reincarnation.]

There simply aren't enough Ghosts around to NOT have reincarnation. It seems returning to another body is happiness.

Prerequisite for Reincarnation

You might ask, "Which consciousnesses reenter a body and which ones simply sleep like the prophet Samuel did?" I don't know the answer to that one. Some say that our creator wants your consciousness to continuously learn things and only after it experiences the things that are required or desired, "it" continues into additional entities. Others say that a consciousness emerges in another body if the previous person had to make restitution for something. Another indicates that it is like a circus. Around and around we go until God calls us home. There are probably a dozen others that you have heard about as well, and I can't tell you what may or may not trigger a reentrance of a consciousness into a new body. There are 4 things that I think I can say about this factor.

- **Death** is not the end.

- **When we die**, our consciousness is released so that it is possible to enter a brand new body.

- **When a body dies** our consciousness or more precisely our soul and spirit may be free to enter an already living body. I assume we would transfer into a young body, which may sound like a baby is not a living soul when it first is born. I'm not getting into that one, because there potentially are more people living today that have ever lived before on the earth so a new born could very well have his soul at conception.

The reason a soul would want to enter a new body is to either learn something special OR to instill happiness or someone is told to. For this book let's just say reincarnation is for Happiness.

Given the above, you might ask is there any proof of reincarnation besides some insecure person not wanting to have to think about death being the end of his existence. The answer is there is. A large amount of written testimony concerning reincarnations and reanimations can be found in the Bible but there is also other proof.

Reincarnation Proof

While there are many, many reports of reincarnated people, Dr. Stevenson methodically documented the child's statements of a previous life gotten from his encounters. After getting details he identified the deceased person the child remembered being, and verified the facts of the deceased person's life that match the child's memory. He even matched birthmarks and birth defects to wounds and scars on the deceased, verified by medical records. His strict methods systematically ruled out all possible "normal" explanations for child's memories that didn't make sense.

Dr. Stevenson devoted well over forty years to the scientific documentation of past life memories of children from all over the world. He collected over 3000 cases in his files alone. Many people, including skeptics and scholars, agree that these cases offer the best evidence yet for reincarnation. Children remembered their past lives. Under hypnosis, others regained knowledge that they could not have had. Some were able to speak in languages they had never learned. On and on and on and on we could go. It is very difficult not to accept this huge database of information that confirms the reincarnation "probability".

Not Reincarnated

Like Samuel in the Old Testament, it reasonable to believe that many consciousnesses do not become reincarnated and stay in some limbo where they can be teachers while people dream or leave there bodies on purpose or leave there bodies to the trauma associated with near death experiences. Certainly, some consciousnesses not associated with living people are sleeping until the time they will be raised and go to another universe and a place called Heaven. Some of the consciousnesses are good and some are not. One thing that is important to remember; all of these consciousnesses are REQUIRED for our universe to exist. We should consider that the consciousnesses [souls] are both all over the place and ready to get us going.

As many released souls return to live again, we must believe reincarnation issues forth a deep seated happiness.

Spirit in a Newborn

For what it's worth, let me just give you my opinion concerning the Spirit and reincarnation. Sometime after conception, once there is some level of liability, a spirit "force" is established in the little one. This holds life to the fetus. This is still not a cognizant entity until a soul enters either from a previously passed person or established another way. I have not reconciled how a soul can be made from nothing, but that does not mean we are all reincarnated, but there is a likelihood that this "released soul" entry is the normal way for cognition.

Do not go thinking I'm saying kill babies for birth control as the souls enter later. While there is a possibility that happens, we also may find that a soul enters fetus very soon after inception. The whole birth process, while being traumatic, may also provide a form of happiness. I know all this sounds bizarre, but true happiness is much different than being happy the food you just bought tastes good. True happiness requires a violation of reality.

Violation of Reality

I have brought out a number of different examples of happiness beyond eating French Fires. The examples I have been presenting are really violations of reality. This does not mean they are not real, nor does it mean we should not attempt to attain these violations of reality. Let me explain it in a slightly different way.

It is reasonable to assume that ultrahigh frequency [Kinetic] light, black holes and the soul are joined by vibrational similarity. We may also assume the carnal life of a tree; the Aether that could eventually make matter, and the potential electric fields [Static] that could eventually do work are joined by vibrational similarity. What I mean by this bizarreness is that everything in the perceived universe is connected in some way vibrationally. If you travel near the speed of light, the only this Real to you are the thing going that speed.

For light to provide a resonance and be sustained, the surrounding vibrational characteristics of the other dimensions must be similar and this is how our soul can modify reality and/or make you happy.

Let me try to explain.

Elimination of Gloom

Let's go slowly. One way this might be attributed is that when we sense the light as **"warm or comforting"**. This is because mass, force and [your life essence] are all in tune. If you bring in gloom, the same sights will become

"Gloomy". In fact, reality around you will be more "depressed". The "power of positive thinking" isn't magic, it is resonance. As you vibrate your soul to a higher, [less selfish, less, carnal way] **you will be happier** and reality around you WILL be brighter as everything in your reality will be vibrating at a higher frequency to all you to experience it. When a majority of the life-forms are resonating at a similar vibration level, they are unified with a perceived reality and each can interact with the other. Becoming too debased and selfish, or too holy changes everything. Those on the debased side are pulled along barely changing reality in any way--- or changing it to be gloomy. Abraham Maslow looked at the other end and found that people who come out of the gloom can become "Self-actualized". By not thinking of self, the self becomes more in control of the environment.

In this book we call control of your environment, Happiness.

If we can vibrate faster, awareness of a higher level of light can bring comfort, insight and understanding. This sounds like all that "power of positive thinking" stuff and it does have some similarity, except that vibrational base is what we call life instead of light.

Life and light are very similar if you have not noticed.

What I mean by this is that visible light is a moving thing. **It goes beyond sight, and extends into comfort, desire, understanding, and awareness.** Light even can "explain" matter because all dimensional dynamos are intricately locked together. As one dimension is stressed outside its normal resonance, the others MUST follow suit. Hopefully this is allowing the whole Anthropics things to sound more feasible as there is a substantial amount of evidence for the controlling element of our consciousnesses building this universe and modifying it.

Particle Resonance

I need to drive this stuff home a little and to do that, let's look at particles.

The difference between a helium atom and a gold atom is vibration, but what keeps the gold atom together? The answer is resonance.

Just like the electro-magnetic resonance, particles express this same feature. Particle resonance is the most comfortable frequency for the Aether [potential for having mass] and gravitational field to stay. It is a point where Aether and gravitational fields both have the same strength and when that occurs, the effect of the 2 fields is most stable. If these two fields are stable at a high frequency, they appear to be a large atomic mass. At lower frequency resonances, the lighter atoms become apparent. You might have gathered from the similarities of the various examples that the esoteric components of life and consciousness would also have this resonance feature and its manipulation can be described and so it does. In this case, a life force and consciousness level would be matched to provide the most stable life pattern.

We might say that changing the resonance of a surrounding is a definition of Happiness.

Continuous Sleep?

Let's take another look a death and see if there is happiness in death. The Bible tells us those who die sleep until the end of days when all will be either judged or will

150

go up to meet God. At the same time it seems to say <u>the instance</u> one dies, he is in the presence of God. The thief on the cross beside Jesus was told that *"this day we will be together in Paradise"*. When Mary Magdalene talked to dead Jesus, three days later he told her not to touch him for *"he had not yet risen"*. [and it had been three days since the thief on the cross died.] All these sound confusing on the surface, but when you add the many comments on reanimation, reincarnation, regeneration, and resurrection, they may sound even more confusing. One thing is certain contact with loved ones after death can make you VERY Happy. Let me start by saying contact is both possible and probable.

Happiness Encounter

My daughter died two years ago. A friend of hers, Cindy, who was closer than a sister called one morning and told us she had seen Wendy in a dream at Cypress Gardens, Florida, with one of their very close High School friends Maury. They were joking around just like they had done while in school and Wendy told Cindy that she was having a great time and not to worry.

While Cindy was still grieving for Wendy a great feeling of joy and happiness was felt for some unknown reason.

The strange part was that Wendy had not seen or had contact with Maury since school. Cindy immediately went on line to find out about Maury thinking she should at least let him know of Wendy's passing. What she found out was that <u>Marty had just died</u> a day before her dream. How weird is that?

There could be a book written just about this type of "Comfort or Happiness encounter". Many have experienced a certain smell of a loved one's cigar, or a glimpse of a departed friend, or a dream of comfort. What I want to concentrate on is, "What does this mean?" Are we ever conscious after we die before the end of time? I know that sounds religious, but I will probably get both highly religious and staunch scientists mad as we investigate this thing together. The first thing we need to understand is that the way we perceive reality has been all wrong.

Trying to stifle things that are not comfortable to our way of thinking most likely will stifle another possibility for happiness.

My Wife

My wife got to be with my daughter for the last year of her life and, was there when she died. The nurse with them could not believe the transition to death as my daughter's face got younger looking and more serene than my wife and this hospice nurse had ever seen. They indicated that Wendy looked like a teenager as she died. Not long after the separation, my wife saw Wendy in sort of a dream wearing a beautiful dress, looking younger, thinner, and happier than she was while alive and Wendy told my wife she was happy. Later my wife got another visitation as she was talking to me on the phone. In a comical way Wendy appeared and told my wife to tell me she had just talked to Wendy. Wendy giggled and told her that I would even remember something like that and then she was gone.

It is not the circumstances or the details, or the time in one of these experiences that is of importance. The thing to figure out here is how and why do these things happen.

Surely, one can decide that it is all in the head, but that does not seem to be the answer.

My belief is that after death a person can try to bring happiness to loved ones. I know sleeping is a big thing in death, but it surly seems like sometimes, and, perhaps, many times the released souls of loved ones try their best to instill happiness by simply being felt by their loved ones or by letting loved one know they are alright.

Because of apparent dependencies on carnal life, living people having difficulty separating themselves from it. Therefore, the soul of a departed 'usually' initiates communication with the dead.

The dead [can]make people happy.

While there are many types of experiences with the dead, there are 2 main types of visions I want to discuss in this book. The first is one we can call **near death visitation** and the second one is **visitation in time of pain**. There are subtle differences in these two but there are also major similarities.

- In both types of instances, the main person that has communication is either the mother or a child. This certainly shows the huge bonds presented in a close family. Occasionally, a close marriage has a spousal visitation, but this is not nearly as frequent as you might think.

- These visions seem to be more prevalent whenever a person is in comfortable surroundings. This could be in a hospital with friends and family nearby, at home or just waking from a dream.

I might suggest here something very bizarre. Sadness begets happiness when associated with the recently departed.

What I mean here is that there is some connection between the newly departed and those closest to them. It seems that the sadder one is concerning their loved ones, the more readily one can gain visitation to bring happiness. It's like a magnet for the newly departed. I'm not suggesting the only way to gain happiness is with extreme sorrow, but it happens.

How Does One Get Happy?

There are a number of steps, but hopefully you are beginning to understand by now.

1. **If you see someone in need help them**. I don't mean give them a dollar, I mean feed, clothe, support, listen to and take up for those needing it. Soon you will become empathetic by the very nature of your soul taking control and BAM! Happiness can fill you before you know it.

2. **Do not worry** about where your food, how hungry you are, or what the food tastes like. Soon, things will not taste as bad and you will not be desiring that 3rd hamburger, your vibrational frequency will increase and the entire world will seem happier to you.---OK it's not quite that simple.

3. **Quit hating**. Once you stop you will soon not be able to hate and you can being a new journey to happiness.

4. **Quit getting mad** if someone does you wrong. Instead find out how you can help them feel better. Not only will your soul be comforted, but you will help someone else begin his journey.

5. **Quit relying on your own knowledge** of something. If you don't worry about it, a wiser answer will be coming. You may not like it as much, but it will be what is right for you and before you know it happiness sneaks in.

6. **For a preacher number 5 even has other bad consequences**. The Bible called this knowledge over wisdom thing "taking the Lord's name in vain" and it was punishable by death. Early preachers would tell others that their sermon was an inspiration of God when they simply "thought" something should be said about something he reasoned out from reading the Bible or looking a raccoons. This use of "knowledge" instead of "wisdom" can be a pretty bad way to NOT gain happiness—especially if someone "stones" you.

7. **Quit primping**. All that does is force you back into the gutter of carnal reality. Why do you have so many mirrors in the first place??? Smashing mirror may help you on the happiness journey.

8. **If you can't stop looking at women, leave places where they are**. This is especially important if you are a woman.

9. **If you are envious of someone who has a Lamborghini don't look**. Get back in you KIA and appreciate what you have. I know this sounds stupid, but it is easy to be happy if you decide to be happy.

10. **If you ever feel sorry for yourself----just quit it**. There are people a lot worse off than you and even if that isn't so, quit it.

11. **If you think it is unfair** that you are not coordinated, can't remember things, are short, awkward, can't spell and you get nervous in front of people. Get over it. I'm getting better about this one; besides, this is just a temporary reality.

12. **Certainly you need to meditate and prayer** is always good. I'm talking about real prayer where you tell our creator that "you will do what he wants" not the "can I get a Lamborghini" prayer.

13. **Self-hypnosis is also good** especially if you use the infratonic audio cues to push your "Self" more into a more catatonic state.

14. **Maslow's self-actualization trick is also good**, but you must succeed in something. Once you have a success, you can more easily ignore the cravings of Self, Sex, and Survival and be able to push "empathy with those around you.

15. Meditation and Prayer- While these are about the same thing. Meditation just doesn't focus on God and prayer does. Here is the thing, **if you want your Spirit portion to help you gain happiness use the prayer one more often** than the meditation one as the spirit is sort of a key to our linked universe, Heaven. [or whatever you want to call it]

16. **If you gain an experience with a dead loved one**, just revel in the love and be filled with happiness of the meeting.

17. **Just simple positive thinking** decreases feeling of dread which increases our happiness.

18. **As I mentioned before visualization of success** regardless of a situation will increase your level of happiness by increasing your vibrational resonance.

19. **Speaking of resonance, going near the speed of light increases your happiness**. By simply spinning in a circle you can do this, but I don't recommend it for beginners.

20. **It goes without say, rejecting Self, Sex, and feeling associated with survival** all increase our happiness.

21. **Apparently seeing the Future** increases happiness. Have you ever seen a sad prophet?

22. **Grow you Pineal Gland** to increase happiness. I don't know how it's done, but make sure it doesn't get too much fluorine.

23. **Adding the "light" to our spirit** increases happiness. Yes, I'm talking about the Holy Spirit

24. **Faith increases happiness**. Certainly the faith to move a mountain is a great type of faith, but as I stated before, faith in our creator may help even more.

25. **Near death experiences** and talking to dead people certainly increase happiness, but don't just talk to any dead guy, find a friend.

The End

About The Author

Steve Preston is a long lime author of scientific, esoteric facts. His books focus on the painful truths rather than whitewashed details that make us comfortable. If you are interested in the truth instead of comfort, please review other works by Mr. Preston as shown below. The images are some from Egypt taking the older version of taxi and in the Negev desert of Israel where the Dead Sea Scrolls were found and near where the beginnings of the Cro Magnon race began.

Searching at Egyptian Pyramid　　　　Searching in Israeli Negev

Kingdoms Before the Flood
Life Resonance
Living on Venus
Lizard People
Make Your Own Global Warming
Man After The Flood
Martians
Meaning of Life and Light
Monsters are Alive
Moses Saved Egypt
Mysteries of the Exodus
Mysterious Pyramids
Mystery of Photons and Light
New look at the Bible
Not from Space
Old Testament Used By Jesus
Our 12-Dimensional Universe
Our Very Odd Presidents
Promote the General Welfare
Races of Men
Releasing Your Consciousness
Retiming the Earth
Scythians Conquer Ireland
Self, Soul, Spirit

Self-Virtualization
Sex Crazed Angels
Six Deaths of Man
Slip Through a Wall
Terror of Global Warming
The Antediluvian War Years
The Antichrist
The Bad Side of Lincoln
The Creation of Adam and Eve
The Devil
The First Creation of Man
The Second Creation of Man
Tracing Cro-Magnon to Jesus
Vampires among Us
Vibrational Matter
Victory of the Earth
Walk Through Time or a Wall
When Giants Ruled the Earth
Where UFOs Go
Why Rome Fought the Berserkers
Why the King James Bible Failed
World War Before
World War with Heaven
World War Zero